THE COMPLETE BOOK

of

FIRE

Building Campfires for

Warmth, Light, Cooking, and Survival

DEDICATION

To my wife Kathleen Hart Tilton. She never lets the fire go out.

THE COMPLETE BOOK

of

FIRE

Building Campfires for

Warmth, Light, Cooking, and Survival

BUCK TILTON

Copyright © 2005 Buck Tilton
All rights reserved
Printed in the United States of America
Published by Menasha Ridge Press
Distributed by The Globe Pequot Press
First edition, first printing

Library of Congress Cataloging-in-Publication Data

Tilton, Buck.
The Complete book of fire : building campfires for warmth, light, cooking, and
survival / Buck Tilton.—1st ed.
p.cm.
ISBN 0-89732-633-4
1. Campfires. 2. Camping. 3. Fire. 4. Survival skills. I. Title.
GV 191.7.T55 2005
796.54'5—dc22

2005047975

◊

Cover design by Travis Bryant
Text design by Clare Minges
Cover photos: lower left by Jef Malon
(www.malon.com)/Alamy
others by Travis Bryant
Illustrations by Scott McGrew

Menasha Ridge Press
P.O. Box 43673
Birmingham, AL 35243
www.menasharidge.com

CONTENTS

INTRODUCTION

"Then the man drowsed off into what seemed to him the most comfortable and satisfying sleep he had ever known. The dog sat facing him and waiting. The brief day drew to a close in a long, slow twilight. There were no signs of a fire to be made, and, besides, never in the dog's experience had it known a man to sit like that in the snow and make no fire. As the twilight drew on, its eager yearning for the fire mastered it, and with a great lifting and shifting of forefeet, it whined softly, then flattened its ears down in anticipation of being chidden by the man. But the man remained silent. Later, the dog whined loudly. And still later it crept close to the man and caught the scent of death."

JACK LONDON, 1902

Jack London's *chechaquo,* a newcomer to Alaska, his mouth sealed shut by the tobacco juice frozen in his beard, died for want of a fire. Some of you will remember from London's classic short story *To Build A Fire* that the dead man had, several hours earlier, set match to a roaring blaze. Using birch bark as tinder, he kindled it carefully with dry grass and small twigs, adding larger twigs and branches as the flames rose. Beside the fire he felt relief from the frigid air and lunched on bacon-filled biscuits. He then walked on into the dark white of the Yukon with his dog, a canine of questionable loyalty. When next he needed a fire, however, he made permanently fatal errors. The dog, I have decided, being intuitively wiser, survived.

Let's assume, and hope, that your fiery needs will never reach life-threatening proportions. But fire has been and will remain a part of your personal history. It has, indeed, been a critical and substantial part of the history of Earth (SEE CHAPTER 1). Say "fire" and mental pictures erupt behind your eyes. The strike of a match, the flick of a Bic, the candle's glow, the mellow warmth of an oil lamp, the flame beneath the mantel, a

windblown conflagration in Yellowstone, a house and the dreams it held
going up in smoke: they're all about fire. Smell the odor of resinous wood
burning, of burning rubber, of steak burned on the grill, and your interest,
and often your concern, is immediately aroused. Convincingly scream "fire,"
and be trampled in the stampede for the exit.

Say "fire," and my mind drifts immediately to a thousand campsites.
The fires burned in circles of blackened stones, in holes dug into the
ground, in sand above an ocean's high tide mark, on log "rafts" floating on
a sea of snow, in fire pans, or beneath U.S. Forest Service grates. These
fires warmed my fingers and toes, dried (and sometimes scorched) my
socks, melted my polypropylene gloves, boiled my morning coffees, fried
my dinners, lit the faces of companions during conversations, and kept me
company all on their own.

What is the magic of a campfire? Why do we want one so badly? Is
it the light, the heat, the inexplicable need to take a perfectly good piece
of wood and make it go away? Perhaps it's in our genes, a tie to a primitive spirit shared by all humans. For thousands of years—and really not
that long ago—fire meant survival, as much a part of daily life as eating
and sleeping. Maybe the magic is something we simply feel? Perhaps the
answer, as with most things mystical and wondrous, will remain forever a
thing for which we have no words.

You may rank among the expert fire builders of our time, or you
may have trouble making flame with a gallon of gas and a blow torch. At
either extreme, or somewhere in between, this book will provide you with
refreshment, enlightenment, and, if I may be bold, entertainment. And
if ever you should really *need* a fire, this book will help you stay warm,
perhaps stay alive.

This book, far more than anything else, is about campfires. It's about
the history and uses of fires in general and campfires specifically. It's about
the size, shape, sound, taste, and smell of campfires. It's about the who,
what, when, where, how, and probably most important, the why of campfires. It's also about cooking on fires, surviving near fires, the destructiveness of fire gone wild, and treating someone burned by fire.

And, fueled by a thousand memories, who knows what else? The
great dark white expanse of the Yukon still lies in wait.

ABOUT THE AUTHOR

Outdoor expert Buck Tilton's respect and knowledge of our mountains, plains, and coastline are embodied in a lifetime of outdoor achievements, including winning the Paul Petzoldt Award for Excellence in Wilderness Education, co-founding the Wilderness Medicine Institute of NOLS, and authoring Leave No Trace's *Master Educator Handbook.*

Buck also knows about fire first-hand. He's battled wildfires on the ground as a hotshot with the Unites States Forest Service and from the air as part of helicopter fire-attack crews. Buck lived in a cabin for 15 years, heated entirely by a wood-burning stove fed by wood that Buck himself cut, split, and stacked. In his lifetime outdoors, Buck has cooked with every conceivable type of stove, but hot coals and flame remain a favorite way to roast or bake a tasty open-air feast.

An experienced author, more than 15 of Buck's books are currently in print, and he is a regular contributor to *Backpacker Magazine.* Buck lives in Lander, Wyoming.

"Some say the world will end in fire,

Some say in ice.

From what I've tasted of desire

I hold with those who favor fire."

ROBERT FROST

CHAPTER 1

A BRIEF HISTORY
of
FIRE

Before men ever dreamed of shelter, campfires were their homes.
Here they gathered and made their first plans for communal living,
for tribal hunts and raids. Here for centuries they dreamed
vague dreams and became slowly aware of the first faint
glimmerings and nebulous urges that eventually were to widen the gulf
between them and the primitive darkness from which they sprang.

SIGURD OLSON, 1956

FROM EARTH'S BEGINNING, and for a long time

after, there was no such thing as fire. Earth's sun "burns," and it is, to put it mildly, hot—about 5,600 degrees Celsius hot. But the heat of our Sun results from nuclear fusion, the same fusion that twinkles in uncounted millions of distant points of light at night. When the Earth spun off from the Sun, it was, of course, mighty hot as well. It was so hot that even 6 billion years later we live on a thin, cool crust floating on a left-over molten core. A few miles below us, amazingly, the Earth is still hot enough to render a human being into ash in a mere second. There's an immense amount of heat and light being produced by the universe, and it has been going on for a staggering amount of time. But none of it, until relatively recently, resulted from combustion—none of the heat and light has been the result of what we know as "fire."

To have combustion, you must have the three components necessary for fire—heat, oxygen, and fuel (SEE CHAPTERS 2 AND 3). Earth had plenty of heat right from the start, but the other two components took billions of years to arrive. Oxygen began to form around 2 billion years ago, 4 billion years after the beginning of Earth, but it didn't reach anything resembling modern levels until about 500 million years back. Even when the Earth first acquired ample heat and oxygen, it still lacked the third component: fuel, something that would burn. Fuel soon appeared, though, in the form of living organisms, vegetable matter with just the right chemistry (SEE CHAPTER 2) to ignite in the presence of heat and oxygen. Combustible plants reached abundant concentrations about 400 million years ago. You can say, truthfully, that life can exist without fire, but fire cannot exist without life. So finally Earth, at the ripe old age of about 5.5 billion years, developed a totally unique (as far as we know) condition in the universe, a condition in which the three essential components of fire coexisted. And then, probably sparked by a lightning strike (lightning still being the most common natural fire starter), up flamed the first fire ever. That happened at least 400 million years ago, and we know that because there is

SOME THINGS
FIRE MADE POSSIBLE:
- *Staying warmer*
- *Cooking food*
- *Drying skin and clothes relatively quickly*
- *Shaping metal*
- *Making pottery and bricks*
- *Keeping wild beasts away*
- *Discouraging pesky insects*
- *Disinfecting water*
- *Signaling with light and smoke*
- *Improving morale*

fossil charcoal dating back that far. For the past 400 million years, maybe as much as 450 million years, there has probably not been a moment without a fire of some sort somewhere on Earth.

But something resembling a campfire could not have occurred until 150 to 200 million years ago. Prior to that time the oxygen content of the air surrounding Earth, always waxing and waning, soared to perhaps as much as 35 percent. With so much oxygen available anything that ignited burned rapidly to a crispy end. Fires were always burning, but they raged powerfully. Somewhere between 150 and 200 million years ago the oxygen content of the air dropped to 21 percent, the percentage of oxygen in the air that still exists today. In air composed of 21 percent oxygen, fires burn at a stable and enjoyable rate. Keep in mind the first surface fire that behaved as a modern Earth campfire was not actually a campfire. The first campfire didn't exist until something nearly human shambled over and camped near it. That event probably occurred between 1.5 and 2 million years ago when, according to fossil records, hominids (our early bipedal ancestors) emerged in Africa.

Undoubtedly pre-humans and early humans rapidly developed a deep appreciation for fire. Near its heat and light, they found safety, not only from cold but also from the jaws of meat-eating predators. Behind the safety of fire, we learned that fire can be used to harden sticks into pointed weapons, rapidly changing us from prey into predator. Fire's light ended the practically useless and fearful darkness of night. Fire dried out the wet—wet skin, wet fur. Its warmth, even though it was unlikely early humans fully realized it, reduced the amount of calories they had to eat to stay warm. When they ate, the taste of cooked meat must have been irresistible. Fire not only cooked food but also rendered some inedible foods, such as acorns and fibrous plants, edible. Fire killed food-borne germs that could shorten a human life. And who can place a value on the psychological comfort of fire? Perhaps its smoky warmth increased not only the joy of living but also the life expectancy of early humans in more ways than are easily counted. It undeniably improved the quality of life immensely.

Once found, fire was guarded jealously. No job was more important or more filled with stress than that of fire preserver. If fire was lost, it had to be found again, an undertaking in which early humans were often left hanging on the whims of nature—the next lightning strike or volcanic eruption—unless it could be taken by force, robbery, or pleading from someone else who had it. But early humans also did not always appreciate where nature had started a fire. They wanted it, for instance, closer to the cave entrance. In order to have a fire where they wanted it, they had to move it. This involved picking up burning material and carrying it to a new spot. You can spend a couple of hours watching the problems this process entailed in the wordless movie *Quest for Fire*. This crude method of "managing" fire went on for thousands and thousands of years.

Evidence indicating when humans were first able to start a fire where they wanted it is scanty. It surely happened at least 14,000 years ago, since ancient evidence of those campfires remains, but it could have happened as long ago as 100,000 years. With the ability to "make" fire, in any case, humans suddenly took a magnificently great leap ahead of all other species. Only we could generate and maintain a fire. It's a monopoly, and the passing of eons has given us no competition.

It is doubtful that any true society of humans, no matter how primitive, ever lacked fire. Shortly after humans encountered fire, fire became the center of human life, a position it held for numerous millennia. Around fires families bonded, tribes banded together, cultures developed, and civilizations arose. The ongoing process of domestication began because fire needed a home, a "dome" to protect and maximize the utilization of fire. Up until the fairly recent past, houses were built with great consideration given to fireplaces and the availability of firewood—then villages, then towns, then cities. When firewood disappeared from a region, entire civilizations sometimes disappeared with it. The Anasazi of the southwestern United States, for example, walked "off the face of the Earth" shortly, say many experts, after the last piece of firewood went up in smoke.

For untold centuries, fire was, and still is, used as a land management "tool." Controlled wildfires burned the vegetation around campsites and villages, creating a firebreak and the safety of a greater field of vision. Deliberate fires drove animals out of dense vegetation where some could be killed for food Animals often returned in greater numbers to the regenerated habitat left by fires.

Fire became a "messenger." It could send signals with light and smoke over long distances. As today, it could be a call for help (SEE CHAPTER 6), a warning, an invitation, or simply a greeting.

Fire, in the presence of human ingenuity, gave birth to science and art. For at least 10,000 years humans have used fire intentionally for purposes other than heat, light, and pointy weapons. The first intentional use of heat to create a product was probably the baking of clay into pottery. When pottery making started is unknown, but the first written record of the use of fire was penned about 5,000 years ago in Sumeria. By 77 A.D., around 2000 years ago, Pliny the Elder wrote in his *Natural History*: "Fire takes sand and melts it into glass. Minerals are smelted to produce copper. Fire produces iron and tempers it, purifies gold, and burns limestone to make mortar that binds blocks together in buildings." Because of fire humans have been able to make magnificent statues, beautiful bowls and cups, and lovely jewelry—to name a few artistic endeavors. The products of almost every civilization, the artistic and the purely functional, have resulted from the application of heat from a fire. The use of fire, pyrotechnology, creates an enormous amount of the products we depend on today (and it may be of interest to note that the pace of life today still results largely from the combustion of fossil fuels).

Beyond the day-to-day necessity of the physical reality of fire, minds burned with thought because of fire. From early on, if there was a ceremony, there was usually a fire. Religious beliefs flamed up around fires. It could be that fire was worshipped even before humans existed as the species we are today. God was fire, or the gods gave fire. For thousands of years, gods have spoken from fire and smoke, and have taken sacrifices from the ashes. Fires purified and carried souls to an afterlife. Sometimes the souls weren't exactly ready to be carried off: heretics, witches, and other suspected heathen were burned at the stake. In places, "eternal flames" soared upward, sometimes for hundreds of years, appeasing the gods, bringing good fortune, honoring the dead. In places, "eternal flames," such as the Olympic flame in Greece and the Kennedy memorial at Arlington National Cemetery, still burn today.

And a fire can do all the things it's capable of doing at once! Fire changed life on earth more than the wheel and the Web. It could be argued that fire made us distinctly human, and the making of fire was the greatest achievement of humans.

CHAPTER 2

"The basis of fire is the physics and chemistry of combustion. Energy stored in biomass is released as heat when materials such as leaves, grass or wood combine with oxygen to form carbon dioxide, water vapour and small amounts of other substances. In some ways, this reaction can be thought of as a reverse of photosynthesis, in which carbon dioxide, water and solar energy are combined, producing a chemical energy store and oxygen."

ROBERT J. WHELAN, 1995

TO MAKE A FIRE requires very little knowledge about what is happening in, let's say, scientific terms. Millions and millions of fires were started and maintained prior to the first doctoral dissertation—and you can burn down an entire forest today with the most meager of educational backgrounds. But in case you are interested in what a fire actually is, this chapter will satisfy your curiosity.

The word "fire," as defined by *Merriam Webster's Collegiate Dictionary*, 11th edition, is "the phenomenon of combustion manifested in light, flame, and heat." Combustion involves oxidation—a chemical reaction in which the hydrogen, carbon, and oxygen in the fuel combine with oxygen from the air that surrounds us. Some oxidation reactions, such as rusting, take a long time. The oxidation reaction in combustion is rapid. Oxidation is an exothermic reaction, and since combustion stimulates rapid oxidation,

FUEL

AIR

HEAT

FIGURE 1: *Fire Triangle*

a lot of energy is released as heat. Light comes from the flame, which is composed largely of glowing particles of burning material. That's the short story—but let's take a closer look at the process.

To make a fire you need air, as a source of oxygen, and you need a source of heat to get the combustion process off and running, and you need fuel to keep the process going. These three elements—oxygen, heat, fuel—are often referred to as the "fire triangle." Without all three sides, you don't have a triangle, and you don't have a fire. In the presence of an adequate amount of oxygen, an adequate amount of heat must be applied in order to ignite the fuel. Combustion occurs when the fuel is raised to its ignition temperature, or "flash point." Once started, combustion is maintained as long as the three elements of fire are maintained.

Just about anything will burn if you raise the temperature of it high enough for long enough. Organic materials, materials that come from some kind of life—trees, bushes, shrubs, grasses, leather, horn—are made mostly of carbon, hydrogen, and oxygen. Organic materials, therefore, are combustible: they will burn. Wood, the fuel of primary concern in this book, begins to decompose when its temperature reaches around 300 degrees Fahrenheit. Some of the decomposing wood rises in the form of volatile gases, compounds of carbon, hydrogen, and oxygen. You may see and call some of these gases "smoke." When the temperature of the volatile gases reaches 572 degrees Fahrenheit, the flash point of wood, the molecules fly apart and the atoms recombine with oxygen to form water, carbon dioxide, and a few other gases. At this point you have a fire, the result of a chemical reaction between two gases—oxygen and the gas from the decomposing wood.

As the fire progresses, the remainder of the decomposing wood becomes either ash, the unburnable materials in the wood (such as potassium and calcium), or char, which is just about pure carbon. The charcoal you light in the grill in your backyard is char, wood that has had almost all the volatile gases removed, leaving you with a mound of carbon. And so you have no smoke from the grill until the burgers start dripping. As it burns, charcoal combines with oxygen, but at a much slower rate than wood, and that's why it stays hot a long time.

Some fuels, such as white gas, burn without forming ash or char. Heat vaporizes the liquid into a volatile gas, and it burns simply as a gas, skipping the decomposition step of wood. Similarly, you are watching the vaporization of wax when you sit beside a burning candle.

Heat is a side effect of the chemical reactions called "fire." Because fire produces its own heat, it is very capable of perpetuating itself. The heat raises the temperature of nearby fuel, more volatile gases are released, the flash point is reached, and the fire continues. Once ignited, as mentioned earlier, a fire will continue as long as you have fuel and oxygen. This fact makes a campfire wonderful—and dangerous. The burden every fire builder must bear, to some degree, is this: Fire has a virtually unlimited power to destroy.

As they heat, unburned carbon atoms, and a few other atoms, give off light. This is the "flame." Flames rise because the gases within it, being hotter and lighter than the surrounding air, are less affected by gravity. That's why fires spread upward rapidly but spread outward much more slowly. Typically described as "red," flame, as you've probably noticed, actually varies in color, with red dominating. The variations depend on the heat of the fire. Where the heat is highest, near the fuel, flame appears blue. Farthest from the fuel, at the "cool" top of the flame, the colors may appear yellow or orange. Colors will vary due to uneven temperatures. Burning fuel other than wood may also produce variations in the color of the flame. (Rising carbon atoms, just so you know, will cool and collect on nearby surfaces, such as the bottom of the coffeepot, as "soot.")

VARIATIONS ON A FIERY THEME

When you choose the materials for your fire, knowledge of certain variables can make life easier. Most of these variables are at least recognized because the knowledge is "common." But here are some facts:

Some materials are more flammable than others. The most flammable materials contain lots of carbon and hydrogen, elements that recombine readily with oxygen to form fire. Even among flammable materials, fuels catch fire at different temperatures. Remember the heat of the fuel must be raised to the point where gases are released, then raised further until the gases react with oxygen. The resin you find in some wood, for instance, has a lower flash point than a chunk of dry, hard, nonresinous wood—resinous wood is more flammable than nonresinous wood (SEE CHAPTER 4).

But it's not just the flash point that is meaningful. The size and shape of fuel also affects the speed at which it burns. A thin twig heats up quickly and thus catches fire quickly. A large tree, on the other end of the wood spectrum, absorbs a lot of heat, requiring a large amount of heat to reach the point where it ignites. After catching fire, thin pieces of fuel burn faster than larger pieces because more of their mass is exposed to the available oxygen. Paper will burn in a "flash," and a thick log may smolder all night long.

With many of your campfires, you'll be concerned about heat production. You need the heat for warmth and/or the food you intend to cook (SEE CHAPTER 7). Heat productivity depends on how fast fuel burns and how much energy the gases involved release—and both of those factors are determined primarily by the fuel being burned. Soft woods, as an example, burn fast and leave poor coals, while hardwoods tend to burn slower into long-lasting, hot coals (SEE CHAPTER 4).

Whether you realize them or not, all of these factors come into play when you make a fire—and that's the subject of Chapter 3.

THE MAKING *of* FIRE

"Beyond the next epoch of geologic time, well after this species has expired and another must examine its record, we may come to be seen as we have often seen ourselves, as a flame—destroying, renewing, transmuting. The Earth's greatest epoch of fire will most likely coincide with our own. Unquenchable fires will have marked our passage. Charcoal will track our progress through history. The flame—tended, suppressed, abandoned—will speak uniquely to our identity as creatures of the Earth."

STEPHEN PYNE, 2001

BEFORE GOING FURTHER, let's acknowledge that fires may be as wanted today, but are certainly not, to put it gently, nearly as needed as they once were, at least in most of the world. Typically no longer a necessity, the making of a fire today must be an ethically responsible undertaking. When you build a fire, you need to build it in an ethically, as well as physically, correct way. Most of this chapter is about the physical act of making a fire, while the next chapter concerns itself with the ethics of fire-making. And since most of the rest of this book has little meaning unless a fire has actually been made, you'll find this chapter the longest.

To combine the three elements—fuel, oxygen, heat (SEE CHAPTER 2)—successfully into a fire requires thoughtful preparation. Here, once again, proof is given to the old adage: "Proper preparation prevents poor performance." And to that list of "Ps" may I add "patience." Almost anyone with a little knowledge can make fire when the conditions are perfect, but a truly great fire builder, one adept at making fire in all conditions, has patience. That person also has a lot of knowledge.

FUEL

Air and the oxygen it contains is all around us, or we wouldn't be here. Assuming you're carrying or you can create a source of heat (SEE BELOW), fuel is the element that requires gathering. Fuels used in starting and maintaining a fire may be divided into three categories: tinder, kindling, and, for lack of a better word, fuel (the long-burning stuff, such as logs).

Tinder is any type of material with a low flash point, a material that will ignite with a bare minimum of heat, sometimes with only a spark. The drier the tinder, in most cases, the more easily it ignites. So important is dry tinder that, not long ago, people carried it in a "tinder box," ready to light when a fire was needed. When you find perfect tinder today, you may choose to carry it in a plastic "tinder bag." Any plastic bag will do. It weighs practically nothing, compresses nicely into pack or pocket, and carrying it will save you time when the half light of evening finds you just arriving at an acceptable campsite.

Dry grasses make excellent tinder that you can find in a multitude of areas. Dry pine needles are also excellent, even though they take a bit more heat to ignite than dry grass. Once pine needles ignite, the resin inside causes them to burn hotter than grass does. Although not as widespread, birch bark is another great source of tinder, but don't rip bark from living trees—collect it from where it has fallen to the ground. The dry inner bark of many species of trees will make good tinder, some of the best being aspen, basswood, cedar, cherry, cottonwood, elm, sage, willow, and walnut.

Tinder may also be, but is not limited to: tiny twigs (if they're dry), the crushed fibers of dry dead plants, small wood shavings, pitch from pine or another sap-rich conifer, crushed fir cones, seed down (such as cattail, milkweed, thistle), wood dust from trees bored by insects, and the lining of abandoned bird and rodent nests. Even in very damp conditions you can often find dry tinder beneath the low-hanging branches of dense evergreens and beneath trees that have toppled almost to the ground. If it happens to be available, you could also use paper, lint, charred cloth, and steel wool. All these things, remember, ignite easily. But instead of trying to memorize a list of species and other things that make good tinder, experiment with what you find in the area or areas where you enjoy camping.

Kindling is the wood used to raise the heat from the burning tinder to a temperature high enough to ignite larger fuel. It, therefore, should ignite with only a little heat. Small, dry twigs make excellent kindling, as does softer wood (SEE CHAPTER 4), especially if it contains resin. You can often find great kindling under coniferous trees where small, dead branches have fallen and been protected by the overhanging living tree. If the wood is about the diameter of a pencil, and dry, it's probably good kindling. Any wood that has been split, should you have the means to split wood, will burn more easily than round pieces, because it's drier inside and more surface of the wood is exposed to the flames. I've traveled in wilderness areas where I was encouraged to split and burn larger pieces of wood due to recent and horrendous windstorms that had choked the forest with downed timber. On most trips, however, larger pieces of wood contribute much to the habitat, and burning them is not recommended. But, where kindling is concerned, a stout knife will split small pieces of wood. And with a knife, one perhaps less than "stout," you can shave off the damp exterior of small pieces of wood to expose the dry inner wood.

The subject of wood as fuel is discussed in Chapters 2 and 4, and to a lesser but critical extent in Chapter 5—and wood will certainly serve as your primary fuel. You may, however, find yourself in want of a fire in regions without adequate wood. Tall, dry grasses may be twisted into thick bunches and burned as fuel. Way down South, I've enjoyed quite a few campfires made entirely of dead palm fronds. Dry animal droppings make an excellent fuel. Remember the "buffalo chips" of the early American West? Dung is, after all, vegetable matter that has passed through a digestive system. In some regions, dry peat, another excellent fuel, can be found beneath undercuts, places where old currents of water have carved into the earth along the banks of streams. Peat is a part of the great biomass of this

FIRE STICKS

You can make kindling from larger pieces of wood, kindling known as "fire sticks" or "fuzz sticks," by partially shaving off "feathers" (small curls of wood), along one-half to two-thirds the length of a piece of wood. Making fire sticks is a tiresome process, but, if you prepare kindling in this way, it will catch fire readily. Place several fire sticks in teepee fashion over the tinder with the "unfuzzed" ends at the top of the teepee.

planet, vegetable matter dead and partially decomposed from contact with air. Dead cacti and other desert plants may be used in arid areas.

When you gather tinder, kindling, and fuel, I strongly suggest you collect at least twice as much as you think you'll need—especially tinder and kindling. If you fail at your first attempt at making fire, you'll be glad you have more material close at hand. What you don't use should be scattered back into the environment, leaving no sign of your gathering.

CHEATING

You may find yourself short on dry material and/or patience, but in possession of several forms of highly flammable fuels, fuels with an intense but short life expectancy. To use such fuels to get a fire started, in addition to more acceptable fuels, is termed by purists as "cheating." Such fuels include, but are not limited to, the gas for your backpacking stove, many insect repellents, and a long list of commercially available "fire starters" that come in forms that include bars, tablets, cakes, and goo you squeeze from a tube (SEE SIDE-BAR, P. 19). If you use gas or another explosive fuel, it must be used with great care. It must be applied only to tinder and kindling and placed prior to the application of heat. NEVER throw gas or other highly flammable fuels directly on flames. Even then, firewood wet with, for example, white gas will literally explode into flame when heat is applied. The application of heat, therefore, must be an undertaking filled with caution. The use of commercial fire starters is, generally

FIGURE 2: *Fire Stick*

speaking, a safe process if you follow the directions on the labels. Note: In a survival situation (SEE CHAPTER 6), when you are concerned not only about making fire but also about living to see the next sunrise, the use of "cheater" fuels is not usually considered cheating.

OXYGEN

Adequate ventilation is mandatory for a fire. A fire won't start without it, and a fire won't keep burning without it. When lots of oxygen gets to the fire—from wind or from you blowing on it—it burns hotter and more brightly. Higher heat from increased ventilation also increases the rate at which the fuel burns. Reduce the ventilation, and the fire burns more slowly. The amount and the degree of heat that comes from a fire, in other words, can be controlled by controlling the air supply to the fire. Furnaces and forges, as examples, work primarily due to control over the air that reaches the fire within. The best campfires have some sort of control over ventilation, such as objects to block wind—and that explains, at least in part, why the United States is littered with uncounted thousands of rock-ringed fire sites.

You can have enough ventilation for a fire but less than adequate ventilation for complete combustion of the fuel. Major results of incomplete combustion are smoke and blackened lumps of unburned wood. You can, in other words, greatly reduce smoke and unburned wood by increasing ventilation.

Incomplete combustion poses much more of a threat than bothersome smoke. Incomplete combustion produces carbon monoxide—an odorless, tasteless, invisible gas. Inhalation of carbon monoxide (CO) causes you to develop a terrible headache, nausea, vomiting, and a loss manual dexterity. Keep inhaling it and you'll become irritable, confused, and, later, lapse into unconsciousness and die from heart failure. CO poisoning from the typical campfire is, frankly, a rare occurrence. But keep CO in mind if your fire is built in a small cave or under a low overhang of stone. A headache and a bit of nausea should send you out immediately into fresh air.

FIRE BUILDING: PART ONE

With tinder, kindling, and fuel gathered and sorted, and a fire site created or chosen (SEE CHAPTER 5), you are almost, but not quite, ready to apply the heat.

The proper preparation of tinder is one of the most critical factors in fire construction. It must be arranged in the chosen site to allow air, and

HOMEMADE FIRE STARTERS

There are numerous homemade fire starters you can whip up in your kitchen before hitting the trail. Here are several:

1. *Coat cotton balls with petroleum jelly (Vaseline, to name a brand). Carry them in a plastic bag or old film canister. They light easily and burn well.*
2. *Pine cones make fairly good tinder, but dipping small ones in hot wax (and letting the wax dry), gives you a bag of fine fire starters.*
3. *Carry some bacon grease in a plastic container. It lights with relative ease and burns hotly (and smells quite good).*
4. *Fill a small paper cup with small wood chips. Pour melted wax over the chips. Allow the mixture to harden, and you have a great fire starter.*
5. *Place lint from your clothes dryer in an empty egg carton. Pour hot wax over the lint, and you end up with a dozen "fuzz balls." Each one will ignite easily and burn for several minutes.*

thus oxygen, to flow around the material. Fluff it up, if it fluffs, and stack it up loosely into the shape of a small volcano.

Over the bed of tinder, stack a small pyramid of kindling. The pieces of kindling should be close enough together for heat to jump easily from one piece to another—but not so close that air cannot circulate freely. If kindling is placed with the pieces separated by approximately one half the width of the pieces of kindling, you have most likely spaced the kindling well. You may also choose to build a second pyramid of larger kindling or smaller fuel over the first one. Of paramount importance, remember, is adequate ventilation. Many a would-be fire has died when heavy wood collapsed on the kindling, smothering the first flames. Leave an opening in the pyramid large enough for you to apply the heat to the tinder. If there is a breeze, the opening should be on the windward side. If it's a strong breeze, one that will extinguish your match or other lighting device, leave the opening toward the leeward side. If wind is hammering camp, don't build a fire (SEE CHAPTER 5).

FIRE BUILDING IN WINTER

Logic suggests that fires in winter—their heat, their light—will be more appreciated than most other times of the year. But from practical and ethical standpoints, fires are more difficult when snow or ice cloaks the ground. Practically speaking, dry fuel is harder to find on a snow-clad winter day. And firewood with its moisture frozen inside makes poor fuel. Ethically speaking, burying ashes in snow temporarily hides them, but the season of melt leaves a pile of evidence on bare earth. When conditions are acceptable in winter, and when you can find fuel, you must build your fire with at least as much, and perhaps more, commitment to making your fire a responsible one. Burn only acceptable fuels, and scatter the ashes broadly (SEE CHAPTER 5). Ashes may look completely messy spread across a white surface, but they'll disappear under the next snowfall and/or when the snow melts.

A further complication of fire-building in snow is finding a proper surface on which to make fire. In shallow snow you may be able to dig down to an acceptable surface. Be certain the surface is free of vegetation (AGAIN, SEE CHAPTER 5). In deep snow you can make fire in a fire pan that "floats" on the surface, or you may be able to make fire on a log "raft," a layer of larger pieces of wood set on the surface of the snow. A fire on a raft, however, presents terribly difficult management problems, primarily concerning the large, partially burned logs left when the fire dies. On ground, pan, or raft, your winter fire should not be built underneath overhanging branches, despite the temptation to sit beneath such a sheltering "roof." Fire can harm or kill the branches, and snow-laden trees may drop a wet load on your flames, leaving you, as was captured in the movie Jeremiah Johnson, suddenly sitting beside a cold heap that moments before was a hot fire.

Due to the ethical complications and practical difficulties, fires on snow are not recommended except in extreme circumstances, such as survival (SEE CHAPTER 6).

COMMERCIAL FIRE STARTERS

Just to give you an idea, here are a few tried and true commercial fire starters:

- *COGHLAN'S FIRE PASTE:* a highly flammable goo you squeeze from a tube, a goo that burns hotly.
- *EASYFLAME UNIVERSAL REUSABLE FIRE STARTER:* a bar you must first soak in a liquid fuel, then light. Once the fire gets going, you can remove the bar, let the heat die, and use the bar again and again.
- *LIGHTNING NUGGET FIRESTARTERS:* small blocks of resinous sawdust and wax that light easily.
- *MAUTZ FIRE RIBBON:* another goo you squeeze from a tube.
- *NATURE'S FIRESTARTER CUBES:* easy-to-light blocks.
- *SAFE LITE FIRESTARTER:* little squares that light easily.
- *SURFLAME FIRESTARTER:* a cup of paper scraps and wood chips mixed with wax that light easily.
- *TINDER-QUIK FIRE TABS:* easy-to-light tablets.
- *WET FIRE TINDER:* small cubes that burn even when soaking wet.

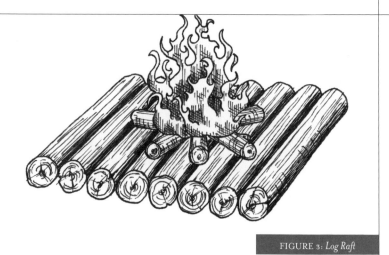

FIGURE 3: *Log Raft*

HEAT: THE PRESENT

Matches have been around for almost 200 years (SEE APPENDIX A). Look at your matches. There's a good chance they're safety matches. A safety match will only light when it strikes against a special surface on the matchbox or matchbook. As with the fire you intend to start, the striking of a match starts a chemical reaction (SEE CHAPTER 2). The head of a safety match is one color, and it's made from a combination of sulfur, powdered glass, and a chemical oxidizing agent. Oxidizing agents are required to keep a flame going once it gets started. The special striking surface is made of sand, powdered glass, and red phosphorus. When you strike a safety match against the match striking surface, friction from the powdered glass produces enough heat to turn a small amount of the red phosphorus into white phosphorus (SEE APPENDIX A). White phosphorus catches fire when exposed to air. The heat from this tiny fire starts a chemical reaction in which the oxidizing agent produces a gas. The gas is oxygen. The oxygen gas and the heat then ignite the sulfur, and the sulfur ignites the wood of the match. It all happens very fast.

Matches in another box could be the "strike anywhere" kind. A "strike anywhere" match has phosphorus on the match head instead of on a special striking surface. The match head will be two colors: one for the phosphorus and one for an oxidizing agent. Other than the fact that you can ignite this match by striking it against almost any surface, "strike anywhere" matches work pretty much the same as safety matches.

A single lighter is worth about 100 books of matches, making one almost infinitely worthy of consideration. If you're carrying a lighter, it's probably one of the ubiquitous, disposable, butane types. When you spin the spark wheel of this lighter with your thumb, the wheel rubs against a piece of flint and produces a spark. Your thumb also depresses a small button or lever that allows butane gas to escape from the lighter. The gas is ignited by the spark. The gas continues to burn as long as you keep the button or lever depressed. Other types of lighters are available (SEE APPENDIX A), some of them excellent fire starters, but the disposable types are inexpensive, dependable, and among the most durable of lighters.

In any case, there is something, let's say, primitively satisfying about applying heat to the well-prepared materials. Strike the match, or thumb the lighter, and set heat to the tinder. (Without a lighter, you can prolong the heat of a match by lighting a candle.) The flames rise, the kindling begins to catch fire, and your efforts are richly rewarded. With the kindling wreathed in flames, gently add increasingly larger pieces of fuel. As you add fuel, place it so that the pieces crisscross each other, assuring sufficient air will continue to reach the growing blaze. The elements—oxygen, heat, fuel—must be kept in balance for your fire to survive.

HEAT: THE PAST

Without the relatively modern convenience of a match, or the modern convenience of a lighter, there are still numerous methods of applying heat to tinder. These methods may be divided into three categories based on the type of device used to create heat. The categories are: 1) fire strikers, 2) fire

MATCH TRICKS

1. *Keep your matches in a plastic bag or waterproof container to keep them dry.*
2. *If you're packing "strike anywhere" matches, arrange them with half of the heads facing one way and half facing the opposite way to reduce the chance they'll rub against each other and ignite.*
3. *You can make your own waterproof matches. Dip a few "strike anywhere" matches into melted wax. Bee's wax works best because it stays soft, but any wax will work—candle wax, for instance, may be dripped onto matches. Allow the waxed matches to dry on aluminum foil. Don't coat the matches too thickly. Thick wax may cause the matches to break when you strike them. If you do end with matches more thickly coated that you wished, leave them as they are until you need them, then gently peel off some the wax with a fingernail before striking.*
4. *Damp matches may be dried enough to work by*

(continued on next page)

MATCH TRICKS (continued)

rubbing one in your hair, if your hair is dry and not too greasy.

5. *Damp matches will sometimes work if you strike one at an angle across the striker strip on a box of matches instead of drawing the match down the length of the strip.*

drills, and 3) fire pistons. Strikers involve one or more of numerous tools that shower sparks on tinder. Drills create heat from friction, from the act of rubbing sticks together. In relation to human history, strikers and drills date back to incredibly ancient times. Fire pistons, a more "modern" tool, generate heat when a piston is rapidly slammed into a small chamber. Although you are unlikely to need an old method, who knows for sure—and they might be fun to try. Some of the most famous old methods are presented here.

FIRE STRIKERS

Some stones will create sparks when they're banged together. It's possible that the first fires ever made were made by using such stones—and iron pyrite and quartz are prime examples. Iron pyrite, sometimes called "fool's gold," looks like gold to the uninitiated. The name "pyrite" comes from the Greek for "firestone." Quartz is the most common mineral on Earth, appearing in many forms and colors, often recognized by its gem-like quality. If you aren't sure you have iron pyrite or quartz, strike two of the rocks against each other and see if sparks fly. These stones—and other silica-rich rocks such as agate, chert, and jasper—will also produce sparks if they are struck with a piece of steel. After the invention of steel, however, flint proved a better spark-producer.

Flint is a hard, even-grained stone found in many regions. It may be white, tan, olive, or blue, but it appears most often as gray, honey-brown, or black. When you strike flint aggressively with a piece of steel, sparks fly freely—sparks easily hot enough to ignite dry tinder. The downside of the flint-and-steel method is this: the spark doesn't last

FIGURE 4: *Knife Showering Sparks from Flint*

very long and, therefore, the tinder must be extremely dry and easily ignitable. You can hold the flint in your hand close to the tinder or place it, if the piece is large enough,

> "Cold night weighs down the forest bough,
>
> Strange shapes go flitting through the gloom.
>
> But see—a spark, a flame, and now
>
> The wilderness is home!"
>
> EDWARD L. SABIN, 1908

on the ground with the tinder nestled against it. You may also choose to nestle the tinder against your booted foot, and hold a smaller piece of flint firmly against the toe of your boot for a firmer grip on the stone. Strike the flint with the blunt edge of your blade if you have a sheath knife. If you have a folding knife, leave the blade folded inside and strike the flint with the blunt edge that protrudes from the handle. Some folding knives have steel caps on the ends. These caps will work just as well—or almost

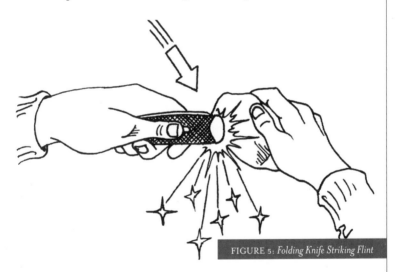

FIGURE 5: *Folding Knife Striking Flint*

as well—as the blade. The strike needs to be a downward, glancing blow to the stone. If you have a saw-edge blade, drawing it across the flint will produce more sparks than striking the flint, but this method does much to dull the edge.

Whether with flint or another spark-generating stone, the hot sparks must fall quickly and directly on dry and fluffy tinder. When you get a small glow from burning tinder, or a thin tendril of smoke, blow gently until flame erupts.

LIGHTER TRICKS

1. *Keep your lighter in a plastic bag. If it gets wet, it won't work until the flint and igniter wheel have time to dry out.*
2. *In cold weather, keep your lighter in an inner pocket to keep it warm enough to function.*

You can buy flint rods, designed for fire building, and flint-and-steel fire-starting kits. Some of these use synthetic flint, the same kind of flint used to create the spark in lighters. You may hear these referred to as a "metal match." These kits may also contain a strip of magnesium, and sometimes the flint and magnesium are mounted together. Magnesium burns hot and fast. Small pieces of magnesium need to be shaved off the strip with your knife and into the tinder. The heat of burning magnesium, ignited by sparks from the flint, will even compensate for a little bit of moisture in the tinder.

BOW DRILL

Methods of applying heat to tinder grow more physically demanding when friction is the source of heat. Therefore they require a lot more preparation time and a lot more practice before you can efficiently start a fire with one of them. Assuming that you haven't started a fire with primitive fire-making tools before (or you probably wouldn't be reading this part of the book), let me encourage you to give it a try. It's a hunk of fun, and the resulting fire is deeply gratifying.

Who knows when fire was first made with a bow drill? That event is long lost in the distant past, but it remains the easiest of the friction methods. With a bow drill, you use friction from a drill rotated on a base (the fireboard) by a bow in order to create first a small pile of wood dust, and then heat to ignite the wood dust. The glowing wood dust is placed on the tinder and blown gently into flame.

You'll need wood for a bow, drill, fireboard, and socket. The wood you choose for the drill and fireboard are of prime importance. Both need to be the same type of wood or at least woods of very similar hardness. If the woods are dissimilar in hardness, one will wear away with friction without producing a hot coal. If you're patient and talented, you can make just about any type of wood work, but choosing wisely can make the job much easier. The wood needs to be relatively hard (SEE CHAPTER 4) for the best results. Of the hardwoods, aspen, cottonwood, sycamore, and willow are examples of woods that work well. I've also had relatively easy work with a yucca drill and a cottonwood fireboard. They are hard, but they are not the hardest hardwoods. The hardest hardwoods, such as oak and hickory, take too much effort. The harder softwoods, such as cedar and tamarack, also work well, but the resinous softwoods—such as fir, pine, and spruce—do not. It is also very important to choose wood that is dry.

The drill, also called the spindle, should be constructed with great care. The drill needs to be a straight piece of straight-grained wood—and the wood must be, as already mentioned, dead and dry. The grain of the wood of the drill, whatever you choose, and to repeat myself, must be straight, and, to repeat myself again, the drill itself must be straight. The length of the drill, for the best results, should be about six to eight inches. Choose a piece of wood about the diameter of one of your fingers, no larger than an inch in diameter. If it's too wide, the drill won't spin fast enough. If it's too narrow, it'll spin so fast you might drill through the fireboard before a spark forms. You need to whittle it off to blunt points on both ends. With a knife, shave off the sides of the drill until you have a rough octagonal shape. You'll be able to create more friction with an octagonal drill than a round drill.

One end of the drill will be placed against a fireboard. The width of the fireboard doesn't much matter , and it only needs to be slightly wider than the width of the drill. It does, however, need to be long enough for you to hold it down with your foot while you work the bow and drill with your hands. When you've chosen a piece of wood for the fireboard, split it in half lengthwise with your knife. All wood was round until it was split to create a flat side. Trim down the split side until it's flat, and trim down the round side until the

FIRE FROM CONCENTRATED SUNLIGHT

Direct sunlight, focused through a lens, can create enough heat to ignite a flame. Fires have acciden-tally started when sunlight was concentrated by shards of a broken bottle onto dry grass or leaves. You once could, and still can on Ebay and at antique stores, pur-chase a "burning glass." In 1803 the Lewis and Clark expedition requisitioned eight dozen burning glasses for its legendary Corps of Discovery. A burning glass is a natural crystal or mag-nifying glass—any lens that magnifies or concentrates, light. You may be able to use the lens of a camera, the lens of a flashlight, or the lens from some compasses. Not having the convenience of premanufactured goods, the Vikings used rock crys-tals as fire starters.

Hold the lens in order to direct the brightest and smallest concentration of sunlight on the tinder. Hold it steady. When a wisp of smoke rises, blow on it very gently until a small flame erupts. "Gently" is the

(continued on next page)

FIRE FROM CONCENTRATED SUNLIGHT

(continued)

operative word here. An old Zen koan poses the thought: "Blow and you can make a fire. Blow and you can extinguish a fire." Add more tinder, then kindling and you know the rest.

FIGURE 6: *Fire from Concentrated Sunlight*

fireboard is about a half-inch to three-quarter-inch thick. Now cut a V-shaped notch into the side of the fireboard, a notch that extends into the board a little more than one-half the diameter of the drill. The V-shaped notch should not be too wide. Make the V about an eighth of a full circle. At the point of the V, gouge out a shallow depression in the board. The depression is where the drill will rest against the board. When you start spinning the drill into the depression, it might kick out of the depression—and that means you've made the depression in the fireboard too close to the edge. You'll have to cut another V and start over. The same hole and notch in the fireboard will usually work for several fires. Once you make a working drill and fireboard, consider hanging on to them.

You'll also need a socket, a piece of wood to hold in the hand you use to hold the upper end of the drill in place. Use a hardwood, if you can, for the socket. (You could also use a rock if it has a suitable depression in it for the drill.) The socket needs to be relatively flat on one side, the side that will hold the upper end of the drill, and it should fit comfortably into the palm of your hand. Gouge out a hole in the flat side of the socket, and take time to make the surface of the hole as smooth as possible. You want to reduce friction in the socket as much as possible. A dab of grease, soap, or some other lubricating substance in the hole of the socket will reduce friction even more. Don't get the ends of the drill mixed up. You want no friction at the socket, and lots of friction at the fireboard.

For the bow you'll need a stiff branch, but one limber enough to be flexed. A branch about 2.5 to 3 feet long and one-half inch to 1 inch in

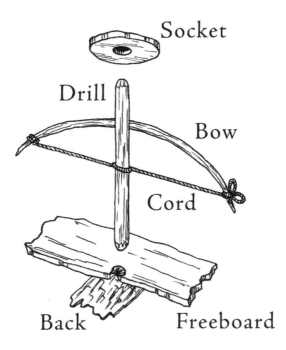

Socket

Drill

Bow

Cord

Back

Freeboard

diameter will work well. Bows too long or too short reduce your efficiency. A length of cordage—a bootlace will work—will be needed to tie both ends of the bow together in order to create the bow shape, a shape very similar to a bow used to shoot arrows. Tie the cord securely to one end of the bow. Use a knot you can easily untie, such as a slipknot, on the other end. The cord typically stretches with use, and you may have to re-tie it to keep tension in the cord. There must be enough tension in the bowstring to maintain tension on the drill when it's inserted into the string. Achieving the right tension usually requires a bit of trial and error. Too little tension, and the drill won't spin. Too much tension, and the drill won't spin.

You're almost ready, but before starting the fire-making process, place a piece of bark beneath the notch in the fireboard. Place a small pile

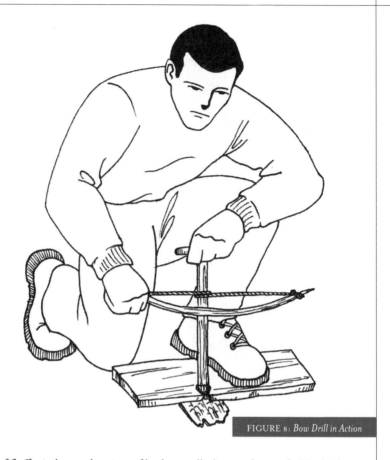

FIGURE 8: *Bow Drill in Action*

of fluffy tinder on the piece of bark as well, close to the notch. The bark will catch the burning pile of wood dust when you tip the fireboard and gently pry out the coal with a knife-tip or sharpened stick. Kneel with the ball of one foot on the fireboard to hold it in place. If the board rocks beneath your foot, whittle some more on the bottom side. The fireboard needs to be held securely in place without rocking. Twist the drill into the bowstring—one twist, one loop of string around the drill. Place one end of the drill in the depression at the point of the notch in the fireboard and the other end in the socket. Brace your socket arm against the leg holding down the fireboard in order to keep the socket securely in place. Maintain downward, perpendicular pressure on the drill.

The downward pressure applied to the drill, plus the speed at which you move the bow, will determine how much friction is created. You'll have to experiment. Too little pressure and you won't have enough friction. Too much pressure and you won't be able to spin the drill. Draw the bow back and forth to spin the drill. Use the full length of the bow with a smooth, fluid motion. Reverse the movement of the bow as quickly as possible. When you change the direction of pull on the bow, each microsecond of idleness means heat is lost. Instead of thinking "fire" when you begin, concentrate on smooth bow action. This is the height of Zen: not the fire that may be only moments away, but the smooth flow of the bow, the steady spin of the drill.

Depending on variables, such as the type of wood you're using and your skill, the drill will seem to spin uselessly at first. Then, as wood is worn away, the end of the drill and the hole in the fireboard will match up in size. The increase in friction will make it more difficult to spin the drill. Smoke, and then wood dust, will begin to appear. At this point, your attention needs to be sharper than ever. Vary the downward pressure on the drill to keep up just enough friction without losing the smooth, full strokes of the bow. Only experience can teach you this. And now is usually the time when the bowstring breaks, or the drill kicks out of the fireboard, or a mosquito bites your nose.

If you endure, the time from the matching up of drill and board until you get a spark is typically less than a minute, often less than 30 seconds. Don't expect to see the spark. What you'll see is a small, smoking pile of wood dust. Now quickly but gently tip the fireboard and spill or pry out the coal. Lift the bark carrying the smoking pile of dust and blow on it very gently or fan it with your other hand. When it starts to glow, place it reverently into the tinder you've prepared, fold the tinder carefully over the glow, and continue to blow. There will be a burst of flame—and you have made fire.

HAND DRILL

Even older than the bow drill is the hand-drill method of making fire. If you've mastered, or at least played with, a bow and drill, you already understand the basic principles involved. You'll be spinning a drill in a fireboard to create friction in order to ignite a small pile of wood dust—but you'll be spinning the drill with your hands. The hand drill takes much more effort than a bow drill.

The considerations you gave to making a drill for a bow drill apply here, but you need a longer drill than the one used for a bow drill. The length depends somewhat on the length of your arms. As you spin the drill, run your hands down the length of the drill in order to maintain

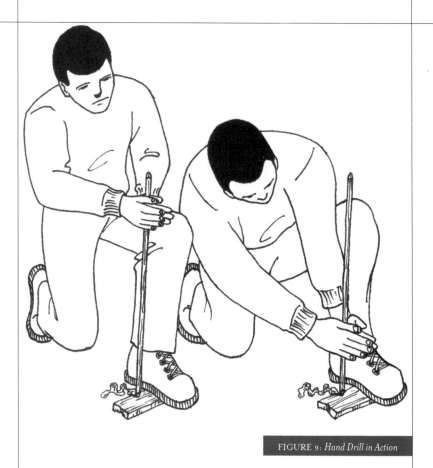

FIGURE 9: *Hand Drill in Action*

adequate downward pressure. The downward pressure maintains the friction. If the drill is too short, you'll stop too often to return your hands to the top—and lose heat. If the drill is too long, the top will whip back and forth as the drill spins, and you'll lose all-important control. A drill about 2.5 feet in length will work just right for many people. If it's a bit too long, that probably won't matter much. A shorter drill will also work, but it takes more skill. Any drill will grow shorter as friction burns off the end in the fireboard. The drill should be less than the diameter of one of your fingers—about a quarter-inch—but it needs to be rigid enough to not bend under the pressure of your downward push. The fireboard for use with a hand drill can be exactly the same as the one you make for a bow drill.

Although I've watched as fire was made efficiently by someone sitting with the sides of both feet on the fireboard, one on each end, I prefer to kneel on one end of the board and spin the drill into the opposite end. It doesn't matter as long as your method works, but kneeling feels more comfortable to me. Whatever your body position, the drill must be kept perpendicular to the fireboard, and your hands must run straight down the drill. Start with the drill between your hands near the top of the drill. Rub your hands together vigorously, spinning the drill back and forth between them. Run your hands down the drill as you rub, maintaining constant downward pressure on the drill. When your hands are about six inches above the board, quickly return them to the top of the drill, and repeat the process. It is very important to return your hands to the top of the drill one at a time. The hand not moving will keep up the downward pressure. If you move both hands at once, the pressure will release from the drill, and air will rush in under the drill, cooling the wood. You'll lose the heat you gained from your previous run down the drill. Expect to tire rapidly so you won't be surprised when you do.

If this sounds simple, I have made a mistake in explaining it. And not only is the hand drill tiring, my first few attempts created rather impressive and painful blisters on the palms of my hands. Early fire builders, with no other means available, undoubtedly developed thickly calloused palms. I've lost count of the number of failed attempts that preceded my first hand-drilled fire.

As with the bow and drill, do not think about fire. Start slowly, learning the rhythm of the drill between your palms. Think smooth action. As your action is polished, increase the speed of your spin and the downward pressure on the drill.

Persistence will eventually lead to smoke, and hot dust, a spark, and, finally, fire. "Persistence and determination alone," said Calvin Coolidge, "are omnipotent."

TWO-PERSON HAND DRILL

With a partner, you can greatly improve the efficiency of a hand drill by either of two methods. In one method, one person, using a socket (SEE PAGE 29), applies downward pressure on the drill. The second person spins the drill between the palms of his or her hands. The one spinning the drill has to talk to the one applying downward pressure in order to adjust the amount of pressure being applied. Without the necessity of applying downward pressure, the spinner can focus on spinning. In the other method, one person performs the typical hand-drill method of spinning the drill, but when the first spinner reaches the bottom of the drill, a second person immediately takes over at the top of the drill. The drill keeps spinning without interruption, and both spinners get a short break while the other spins.

MOUTH-AND-HAND DRILL

A somewhat risky alternative to the hand drill is the mouth-and-hand drill. You spin the drill between your hands, but you supply downward pressure with your neck muscles by holding a socket **between your teeth**. The length of the drill will depend on the length of your torso, but a drill about 2.5 feet long works for most people. And remember the drill needs to be straight! Of critical importance is the socket you hold in your mouth. To keep the drill from slipping out and jabbing you in the face, the socket needs to big enough but not so big you can't hold it firmly in place with relative comfort. A socket about two inches wide will probably work. You

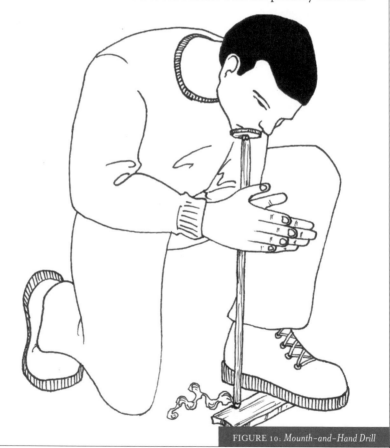

FIGURE 10: *Mounth-and-Hand Drill*

can make one by splitting a piece of wood about two inches in diameter. On the flat side gouge out a hole as you did with the socket for a bow drill. Whittle away at the rounded side of the socket until it fits your mouth. The more teeth you can bite with the better. If you think the other friction methods demand practice, this one needs the most. Approach trials with great care. The teeth you break out, or the third nostril you tear out, could be your own.

FIRE PLOW

You have seen the fire plow in action if you've seen the movie *Cast Away*. This method, like the bow and drill and hand drill, works by creating friction. And once again you'll need a drill and a fireboard. The drill does not have to be perfectly straight and the fireboard is usually easier to manage if you make it larger than the one you made for the other two methods. Cut a groove down the middle of the fireboard. By applying pressure to the drill while you run it aggressively down and up the groove, you can create a pile of wood dust that will eventually ignite. As with the other methods, failure to create wood dust probably means you've chosen too hard a wood for the board.

You'll need to work the drill with both hands unless you're unusually strong and/or determined. The drill should be kept at approximately a 45-degree angle to the board. The board can be laid flat on the ground, but

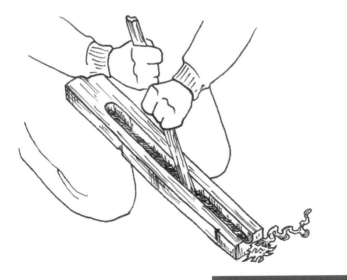

FIGURE 11: *Fire Plow in Action*

propping up one end of the board, against a piece of wood or your thigh, gives you a better working position. Remember, the surface of the groove and the end of the drill must match up in size before suitable friction develops. You can make a fire plough more efficient by taking the time to cut the groove to match the end of the drill. But no matter how much time you spend cutting and smoothing the groove, and shaping the end of the drill, you'll still expend quite a bit of effort rubbing the drill into the fire-board before enough friction is generated. Once the materials are gathered, the primitive tools made, and the basic procedure understood, it will be patience and persistence that bring the reward of fire.

FIRE PISTON

The origin of the fire piston, even though it's a much more modern tool, is shrouded in mystery. For sure, fire pistons were known in France in 1802 and in England in 1807. It is probable, however, that they originated somewhere in Asia—Indo-China for instance—from a relatively primitive people prior to the piston's "discovery" in Europe. In any case, the use of fire pistons was widespread by the mid-1850s.

Remarkable in its ingenuity and construction, a fire piston requires three essential components: a cylinder with a precise bore, a piston that perfectly fits the bore of the cylinder, and highly flammable tinder. Materials for making effective cylinders and pistons have included wood, bamboo, horn, ivory, bone, brass, and lead. The average size of a cylinder is 3.25 inches long and a half-inch wide, with a bore size of three-eighths of an inch. Larger ones, say the experts, don't work well, and smaller ones don't work at all. Although simple to operate, the construction of a fire piston would have been an enormous challenge, which adds considerably to the mystery of from where the first one came.

A fire piston operates on the same basic principle as a diesel engine. Air is forced into the cylinder by rapidly depressing the piston. The speed of the piston compresses the air and creates heat. Heat comes from

FIGURE 13: *Fire Piston*

friction, the friction of the molecules of air being compressed. The heat ignites a small ball of tinder tucked into a cavity in the bottom of the piston. The piston is quickly withdrawn, and the glowing ball of tinder is picked out—a sharp piece of stick will work well—and placed in a pile of tinder.

For maximum efficiency, the cylinder is typically held firmly in one hand, and the piston, with a small piece of tinder stuffed into the little depression at the bottom of the piston, is started into the mouth of the bore. A quick and sudden stroke with the other hand, and the piston is depressed. The piston will rebound slightly from the pressure of the compressed air. If the piston is instantly removed from the cylinder, the tinder is lit and ready for use.

FIRE BUILDING: PART TWO

Once your fire is up and going—the tinder consumed, the kindling ablaze, smaller fuel added and ignited—you can, and maybe have, maintained a fire by simply adding more and larger pieces of fuel. This usually works fine as long as you add fuel in a crisscross fashion to maintain an adequate air supply. The way you add larger fuel to a fire is sometimes called the lay of the fire, and different fire lays serve different needs. Some of the most common are presented here:

A teepee fire, shaped like a teepee, sheds good light and concentrates the heat above the apex of the teepee, allowing you to boil water fast in a pot suspended over the apex. The teepee of fuel is most easily built if you push a stick into the ground securely, slanting it over the flames. Then lean a circle of sticks against the stick with its end buried in the ground. If a breeze is blowing, leave a "door" in the teepee on the windward side. Keep adding fuel to the teepee until your fire has reached the size you desire. On the down side, teepees tend to fall over eventually, but they are generally the easiest lay of fire to get going, and so they make great starter fires.

FIGURE 13: *Teepee Fire*

A log cabin fire, shaped roughly like a tiny log cabin, creates great light and heat, largely because the fire

FIGURE 14: *Log Cabin Fire*

gets a lot of oxygen. In a log cabin lay, the fuel is stacked like the walls of a cabin, with the interior space open for tinder, kindling, and small fuel. Because they burn hot, log cabin fires create a large bed of coals fairly quickly, a plus if you plan to cook on coals (SEE CHAPTER 7). Since they produce great light, log cabin fires also work well as signal fires (SEE CHAPTER 8).

A pyramid fire looks similar to a log cabin fire except you build layers of fuel over the flames instead of a hollow framework with the fire inside. Each layer is a bit smaller than the previous layer, thus the pyramid shape. This construction has a couple of advantages: 1) the fire will burn a long time, a good thing if you want the light and heat for, say, an overnight flame, and 2) damper wood can be placed near the top, and the heat will dry it before you need it as fuel.

A star fire looks sort of like a wheel without the rim. The fuel is the spokes of the wheel, and the fire burns at the hub. Star fires do not create a lot of light or heat, but they work fine when you don't need or want a large fire and/or when you need to conserve fuel. The pieces of fuel are pushed into the fire as the ends burn off, so a star fire requires almost constant attention.

PUTTING THE FIRE TO BED

Most of the time, you'll want your fire to die completely during the night. In the morning, with the addition of water, for safety's sake, and the judicious scattering of wet ashes and other remnants of your fire, you can walk away

FIGURE 15: *Pyramid Fire*

leaving no sign of your conflagration (SEE CHAPTER 5). But there may be times when you'll want to wake to hot coals and brief work to return the fire to abundant life.

Unfortunately, there is no sure way to guarantee you'll have hot coals in the morning without getting up once or twice in the darkness and adding fuel. But there are steps you can take to give your fire the best chance possible of surviving the night.

Before hitting the sack, build up a bed of hot coals and "bank" them. To bank coals means reducing them to a slow-burning bed of smoldering heat. Rake them into a mound. A well-banked bed of coals, especially

FIGURE 16: *Star Fire*

hardwood coals, will often burn eight hours or more. Soon after rising, spread the mound to find the heat, add tinder and kindling, and soon a fresh fire blazes.

You can bury hot coals under pieces of wood larger than you'd usually put into your fire. With plenty of fuel to eat at slowly, a fire may burn, of course, for days. A fire left to burn actively all night must be situated safely, the fire site chosen with great care (SEE CHAPTER 5). Don't do this unless you're willing and able to take the time to burn large chunks of wood completely to ash in the morning—and there will always be large blackened chunks of wood left after an all-night fire.

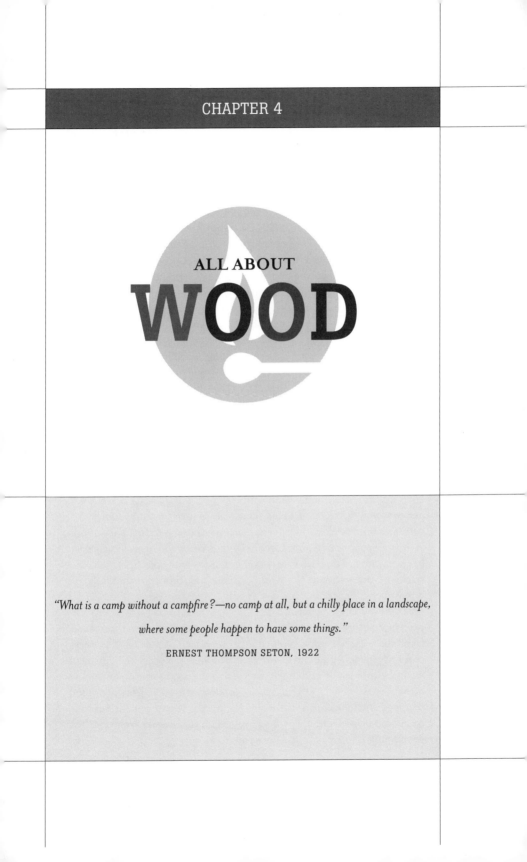

CHAPTER 4

ALL ABOUT

WOOD

"What is a camp without a campfire?—no camp at all, but a chilly place in a landscape,
where some people happen to have some things."

ERNEST THOMPSON SETON, 1922

DEBATES RAGE, or at least simmer, concerning what species of tree produces the best wood for a fire. Science and personal opinion aside, the bottom line, and by far the most important aspect of gathering fuel, is this: use the type of trees that provide abundant firewood near where you're building your fire. And, also important, choose dry wood. Wet wood, no matter the type, always makes a poor choice for firewood. The wood may feel dense (good), but much of the weight is water (bad). A large amount of the heat energy from your fire will be consumed drying out wet wood before it reaches its ignition temperature. Too much wet wood will, in fact, kill an otherwise healthy fire. And wet wood does not burn completely, creating a heap of pollution. "Green" wood—wood, in this context, still growing or very recently growing—is extremely wet. Sixty percent or more of the weight of a living tree is water. Like a human being's, a tree's main ingredient is water.

As you're gathering firewood, keep in mind that dead wood, even when dry, may be too dead. Crumbly, "punky" wood is of no service as good firewood—plus it's well on its way to being naturally recycled as nutrition for living plants (SEE CHAPTER 5). If you can push your thumbnail easily into a piece of wood, it's too rotten to use. Leave it alone to continue its journey on the great circle of life.

As with Chapter 2, you don't need any more information from this chapter to build a nice fire. But you can keep reading to learn a lot more about wood.

As wood dries out, it "seasons." Many variables determine how long it takes for wood to season. Wood with intact bark dries much slower than peeled wood. Firewood, the bark intact, cut to stove length and stacked beside your house, loses most of its moisture through the cut ends. It takes at least nine months, if air can get to it, for green wood to season after it has been cut and stacked. It may take as long as two years. Splitting and stacking wood decreases drying time. Interesting, though, is that fully dried wood is not technically "dry." It only has to drop below 25 percent moisture content to be termed "dry." Well-seasoned wood still retains a 20-percent moisture content. To put it another way, a piece of well-seasoned wood that weighs 5 pounds (80 ounces) represents 4 pounds (64 ounces) of wood fiber and 1 pound (16 ounces) of water. You want well-seasoned wood for your campfire, but you won't have any way to measure the moisture content—you'll just know you're picking up dead and downed wood that feels and looks dry. You can also test the dryness of wood when you break it. If it snaps cleanly with a crisp sound, you're most likely now holding a couple of pieces of good firewood.

There are, however, substantial differences in types of wood. The major differences in species, in relation to fire, lie in the density of the wood. Denser wood, generally speaking, has more latent heat energy ready to be released when the wood burns. Due to many variables, measuring latent heat energy is an imprecise science. When the air is humid, for instance, you're going to lose some heat energy from the wood in your fire (SEE CHAPTER 8). But we can still categorize and rank woods according to available heat energy within a standard unit such as the pound or kilogram.

The softwoods—consider pine, spruce, and cedar—are less dense. A cord of well-seasoned cedar, one of the least dense woods, might weigh as "little" as 1,900 pounds. Softwoods ignite more easily and burn relatively fast compared to hardwoods. They give off a lot of light, but they make less heat and relatively short-lasting coals. A soft, dry wood makes fair-to-good firewood, and a good-to-excellent kindling, depending on how resinous the wood. You can often see, smell the sweet aroma, and/or feel the tackiness of a wood's resin. Even though softwoods tend to hold resin, and resin increases latent heat energy, the density of hardwoods still gives them more heat energy than softwoods. Softwoods also tend to "pop" and throw off sparks, especially the more resinous woods, and hardwoods tend toward the opposite. The hardwoods—oak, maple, and hickory, to name three—are much denser than softwoods such as cedar or pine. A cord of well-seasoned hickory, one of the densest woods, may weigh in at over 4,300 pounds. Hardwoods are more difficult to ignite and burn slower, producing a lot of heat and long-lasting coals. Since hardwoods vary greatly in density, they are sometimes divided further into

A CORD OF WOOD:
You'll never cut a cord of wood for your campfire, but you might want to be able to answer this question: What is a cord of wood? A "cord" refers to the volume of the wood. Historically, a stack of wood four feet wide, four feet high, and eight feet long is called a "cord of wood." If you do the math, you get a volume of 128 cubic feet (4 x 4 x 8 = 128). But due to the air spaces between the stacked pieces of wood, the actual volume of wood in a cord, according to the U. S. Forest Products Laboratory, runs around 85 cubic feet. The weight of a cord of wood depends on the density of the specific wood and how seasoned the wood is. The least seasoned cord will weigh is a bit less than one ton (2,000 pounds), but some woods weigh in at over two tons per seasoned cord.

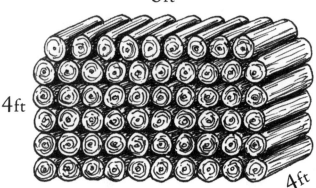

"medium hardwoods" and "hardwoods." The medium hardwoods—such as alder, aspen, cottonwood, maple, and sage—fall between softwoods and hardwoods in their ease of ignition and speed of burn.

You don't need to be a dendrologist, or even a botanist, to distinguish softwoods from hardwoods. Softwoods are evergreens, needle-bearing trees. Hardwoods are trees that have flat leaves, which are cyclically shed. (Willows, just to note, are somewhat puzzling trees, bearing flat leaves but having some characteristics found in softwoods, leaving experts divided on whether the willow is hard or soft.) When you find dead wood on the ground, look up at the living trees from which the dead wood fell.

In an ideal fire-building world, to sum up, softwoods tend to make fine kindling and hardwoods the best fuel (SEE CHAPTER 3). For a specific look at the variations of types of wood with respect to their potential as fuel for your fire, see the Wood Chart on the facing page.

The following information is based on research by the U. S. Forest Products Laboratory and New Mexico State University Cooperative Extension Service, fueled additionally with a few sticks of personal experience.

WOOD CHART

HARDWOODS

NAME OF TREE	HEAT	EASE OF BURN	REMARKS
Apple	High	Poor	Good firewood, small flame, nice aroma.
Alder	Low	Good	Poor firewood, burns fast.
Ash, Black	Medium	Fair	Good firewood.
Ash, White	High	Good	Excellent firewood.
Aspen	Low	Good	Fair firewood, good for kindling.
Basswood	Low	Good	Fair firewood, good for kindling.
Beech	High	Fair	Good firewood, tends to throw off sparks.
Birch, Black	High	Good	Good firewood, but burns fast.
Birch, Gray	Medium	Good	Fair firewood, but burns fast.
Birch, Paper	Medium	Good	Fair firewood, but burns fast.
Birch, White	Medium	Good	Fair firewood, but burns fast.
Birch, Yellow	High	Good	Good firewood, but burns fast.
Cherry	Medium	Fair	Fair firewood, burns slow, nice aroma.
Chestnut	Low	Fair	Poor firewood, tends to throw sparks.
Cottonwood	Low	Good	Fair firewood, good for kindling.
Dogwood	High	Good	Excellent firewood.
Elder	Low	Good	Poor firewood, burns fast.
Elm, American	Medium	Fair	Fair firewood, burns slow.
Elm, White	Medium	Fair	Fair firewood, burns slow.
Gum	Medium	Fair	Fair firewood.
Hackberry	Medium	Fair	Fair firewood.
Hawthorn	High	Fair	Good firewood.
Hemlock	Low	Fair	Fair firewood.
Hickory	High	Good	Excellent firewood.
Hornbeam	High	Good	Excellent firewood.
Locust	High	Poor	Fair firewood.
Maple, Hard	High	Good	Excellent firewood.
Maple, Soft/Red	Medium	Good	Good firewood.
Maple, Sugar	High	Poor	Good firewood, once it starts burning.
Mesquite	High	Fair	Good firewood.
Oak, Red	High	Poor	Excellent firewood.

WOOD CHART (continued)

	NAME OF TREE	HEAT	EASE OF BURN	REMARKS
HARDWOODS	Oak, White	High	Poor	Excellent firewood, once it starts burning.
	Pecan	High	Good	Excellent firewood.
	Sycamore	Medium	Good	Good firewood.
	Walnut	Medium	Good	Good firewood.
	Willow	Low	Fair	Poor firewood.
SOFTWOODS	Cedar	High	Good	Good firewood, great kindling, nice aroma.
	Cypress	Medium	Fair	Fair firewood.
	Fir, Balsam	Low	Fair	Poor firewood.
	Fir, Douglas	High	Good	Good firewood, small flame.
	Juniper	Medium	Good	Good firewood, great kindling, nice aroma.
	Larch	Medium	Good	Fair firewood.
	Pine, Jack	Low	Good	Fair firewood, good for kindling.
	Pine, Norway	Low	Good	Fair firewood, good for kindling.
	Pine, Pinon	Medium	Good	Good firewood, excellent kindling.
	Pine, Pitch	Low	Good	Fair firewood, good for kindling.
	Pine, Ponderosa	Low	Good	Fair firewood, good for kindling.
	Pine, Sugar	Low	Good	Fair firewood, good for kindling.
	Pine, White, Eastern	Low	Good	Fair firewood, good for kindling.
	Pine, White, Western	Low	Good	Fair firewood, good for kindling.
	Pine, Yellow	High	Good	Good firewood.
	Poplar, Yellow	Low	Fair	Poor firewood.
	Redwood	Medium	Fair	Fair firewood.
	Spruce	Low	Good	Fair firewood, burns fast, lots of sparks.
	Tamarack	Medium	Good	Fair firewood.

"*Wood already touched by fire
is not hard to set alight.*"

AFRICAN PROVERB

CHAPTER 5

TO BUILD —
or
NOT TO BUILD —
a
FIRE

"*Now, with new knowledge and viable conservation practices, there is no excuse*
for an individual or group to harm the land or the ecosystem
in primitive areas to the detriment of future generations."

PAUL PETZOLDT, 1974

DESPITE THE APPEAL and usefulness of campfires, this fact, as mentioned before, remains: you seldom need one. Once essential for food preparation and sometimes comfort, you can now use a lightweight stove and wear adequate clothing properly (and eat well) to maintain body temperature.

Careless use of fires and the indiscriminate gathering of firewood have ruined the natural appearance of many popular recreational areas and otherwise pristine wilderness areas. Rings of blackened rocks, sometimes massive, filled with mountains of ash, partially burned logs and trash, are, to say the least, unsightly—and the impact is lasting. Long after the trampled grass grows back, even after trees have sprouted in your footprints and reached maturity, the scars of a fire site will remain. A large, hot fire sterilizes the soil to depths that may reach four inches or more.

What's left, not noticed at first, is a wound that refuses to heal. Even less noticed at first is the fact that downed wood, allowed to decay into the soil instead of being consumed in a fire, is a significant part of the natural cycle of life. Decayed wood holds more water than soil in times of drought, and rots into nutritional elements necessary to keep soil productivity high. Poor campfire management has, and probably will continue to, set off terribly destructive wildfires (SEE CHAPTER 8). You can often, however, enjoy a campfire while avoiding a lasting impact. You need thoughtfulness, attention to details, and prior planning and preparation.

Build a campfire only when environmental conditions allow it. The danger of wildfire must be low, and you can find out if it is by checking with land management agencies: state and federal forest and wildlife services, Bureau of Land Management offices, and state and National Park Service offices. Land managers will also be able to tell you if there are specific regulations governing the use of fires.

In some places and/or in some seasons, fires are not allowed. As an example, more than 40 percent of our national parks currently prohibit campfires. When they are allowed, sometimes specific fire-building and fire-managing guidelines must be followed. You should also use common sense. High winds casting sparks over alarming distances are shouting "no fire tonight!" even when other conditions are met. Dead and downed firewood, in every case, must be plentiful (SEE BELOW). You must have plenty of time to prepare the fire site, thoroughly extinguish the fire, and, in many cases, hide all evidence that you were roasting marshmallows only an hour earlier.

THE FIRE SITE

If conditions are "go" for a fire and a fire grate or fire ring already exists, use it. An established fire site is actually a bonus: less fire site preparation time is required, and less clean up time is necessary. Not long ago, I arrived at one high-use campsite in Colorado's Gunnison National Forest to find five fire rings. When I left there was one fire ring. There is rarely a reason to build a fire ring, and there is no reason to build a fire ring if one is waiting. Dismantling and removing signs of unnecessary fire rings is certainly not mandatory, but it feels like a nice thing to do. Leaving one fire ring of reasonable size, on the other hand, encourages future fire builders to use it. Leave it without trash and without a mound of ash and unburned logs.

NO-FIRE ZONES:

There are fragile environments where conditions may appear to say "build a fire," but, on closer inspection, they are not. Arctic willows and alpine krummholz, for instance, represent plants that grow with extreme slowness. They need the soil replenished by their fallen, dead limbs. A campfire of dead wood will blaze for a few minutes with those plants, and new growth will require, literally, centuries to reach maturity, die, and fall. Fire up the stove, and leave the wood.

FIGURE 18: *Old Fire Ring*

You may find an old fire site without a ring of stones, a spot thoroughly blackened by previous fires. These spots are acceptable sites for new fires. If the fire site is covered with loose forest debris—small twigs, needles, leaves, sprigs of dead grass—gather them into a pile to use for tinder, or scrape them gently away, at least five feet away. Burn, in other words, only what you fully intend to burn. After the fire, scatter the cold ash (SEE BELOW). Leave the site in better condition than you found it.

When you are in a pristine area and no fire site already exists, choose a site that you can walk away from without leaving a trace. You can scoop out a shallow depression in sand or gravel along the shorelines of seas and rivers. Without a beach, you can dig a shallow pit for a fire in sandy, rocky, or gravelly ground that has no overlying vegetation, no underlying roots, and no nearby dry grasses. Even if you are well away from a tree, you may still find yourself under overhanging branches, and you should not build a fire there. The heat may rise high enough to scorch or even kill the branches. After the fire, after removing and scattering all the ash, you can fill in the depression or pit. Don't just bury the ash. It'll eventually work its way to the surface.

If you've planned ahead and prepared, you can build an environmentally acceptable fire even when you can't find a completely acceptable site. The details of two such methods are below:

MOUND FIRES

Minimum impact fires can be built on mounds of sand, gravel, or mineral soil (soil with a low organic content). Finding the appropriate sand, gravel, or soil for the mound is usually the problematic task. Look where fallen trees have exposed the underlying soil and in dry streambeds. You'll have to haul the material for the mound to your fire site, which can be just about anywhere if the mound is thick enough. But building the mound on a durable site—rock, sand, bare ground—will reduce the chance of an impact. Haul the material in your sleeping bag's stuff sack, turning the sack inside out first to keep dirt off the inside. A trowel or small shovel will aid greatly in gathering the material. Build the mound on a ground cloth or fire blanket—not necessary but it sure makes clean up easier because you're going to be returning the mound's material to its source and broadly scattering the ash. A cloth or blanket about three feet by three feet will be adequate in size. Make the mound six to eight inches thick to protect the cloth and/or the surface beneath, and make it about two feet in diameter. The cloth can be rolled up under the edge of the mound to prevent sparks and embers from burning or melting it.

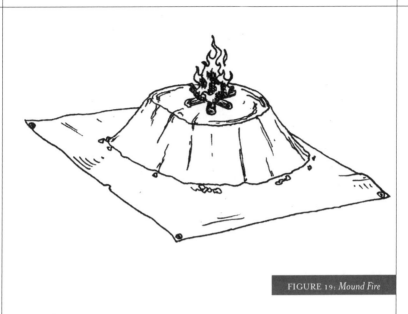

FIGURE 19: *Mound Fire*

Fire Pans

For even less impact than a mound fire, carry a fire pan. A fire pan can be anything metal: commercial fire pans, oil pans, aluminum roasting pans, garbage can lids. The pan needs to have sides high enough—three inches

FIGURE 20: *Fire Pan*

RESPONSIBLE FIRE-BUILDING:

- *Assure an abundance of firewood.*
- *Make a safe fire.*
- *Keep the fire small.*
- *Minimize long-lasting impact to the site.*
- *Make sure the fire is thoroughly out.*
- *Erase evidence of the fire.*

will be enough—to contain the fire. Place the pan on a durable surface, and elevate it on a few rocks to prevent damage to vegetation and soil below. Fill the pan with a couple of inches of inorganic soil prior to building a fire, and you're ready to go. In the morning, you can drown the ashes and easily disperse them over a large area by scattering them from the pan.

THE FIRE'S WOOD

The best firewood, environmentally speaking, is the dead and downed stuff lying at least relatively close to your fire site. (SEE CHAPTER 4 TO LEARN MORE ABOUT WOOD.) Don't break branches from trees, dead or living, a practice that scars the forest. Pick up sticks you can break with your hands, sticks no larger than one or two inches in diameter. Wood too difficult to break ranks higher in its value to the ecosystem. You may find chunks of dry, rotten wood that will burn okay, but, once again, leave it for the plants and animals of the forest. Gathering smaller pieces of wood will also encourage you to keep your fire of a reasonable size, which is small. Smaller wood pieces burn easily and completely to ash, making clean up easier and the results of your clean up better. Half-burned logs are ugly and a huge disposal problem. Even though you just hiked ten miles to reach the back of beyond, walk well away from camp—start, say, 100 yards out—to gather the wood, leaving the immediate vicinity appearing less impacted. A few, rare wilderness areas are trying to reduce extensive amounts of dead wood, and suggest you carry a saw, ax, or hatchet—otherwise save the weight . . . and the wood.

BURN ONLY WOOD

Plastic doesn't burn. It melts, contributing to air pollution. Foil and foil-lined packages won't burn. Leftover food requires high heat for a long time to burn. Other than paper, burn only wood.

CAMPFIRE MANAGEMENT

There is no safe way to leave a fire unattended, so never do it. Stop feeding the fire an hour or so before you plan to clean up, allowing time for the wood to burn completely. As the fire burns down, add the unburned stick ends. When the heat nears its end, crush any bits of charcoal into powder. Your goal is a pile of white ash and black powder—and nothing more. For those who care about minimum impact, the greatest contributing factor to a lack of success is failure to give yourself time to restore a site to its original (or better) state. Haste, in other words, makes impact.

For reasons related to haste, morning fires are usually a poorly conceived idea. The fire that died the night before will have lost its heat, the addition of a lot of water is often not needed, and clean up is fast and easy.

When all you've got is ash and powder, saturate the remains with water, stirring everything up well to make sure the heat is completely gone. The ash must be cool to the touch. To know if this is true, you'll have to touch the ash, running your fingers through it. Rummaging through the remains allows you to remove anything unburned. Even if it's not your unburned trash, remove it, and pack it out. With a small shovel or trowel—or a pot lid if you need to improvise—widely scatter the ash. The larger the area over which you scatter the ash, the smaller will be the signs of your fire.

Finally, restore the appearance of the fire site. If you've used a fire ring, scatter your ash to leave the site ready for the next visitor. If you've scooped out a pit, fill it in. If you've hauled in soil for a mound, haul it back. If you've gathered more firewood than you need, broadcast it widely back into the forest. As Zen master Shunryu Suzuki said, "When you do something, you should burn yourself completely . . . leaving no trace of yourself."

THE SEVEN PRINCIPLES OF LEAVE NO TRACE (WWW.LNT.COM)

1. *Plan ahead and prepare.*
2. *Travel and camp on durable surfaces.*
3. *Dispose of waste properly.*
4. *Leave what you find.*
5. *Minimize campfire impacts.*
6. *Respect wildlife.*
7. *Be considerate of other visitors.*

CHAPTER 6

THE SURVIVAL FIRE

"Firecraft comes third in my hierarchy of needs, because if you've got clothing and shelter, you may not need the fire. The ability to build a fire is a tremendous physical and psychological boost. On the other hand, if you think you're a good outdoorsman and can't get a fire going, that can be a very heavy burden to carry, a real downer."

PETER KUMMERFELDT, 1999

TO BEGIN, and to make sure we're all on the same page, let's define a survival situation. It is not when you're uncomfortable, or even when you're miserable. You're in a survival situation when there is a clear and present threat to your life. If you don't take the appropriate actions, and even if you do, you might die.

This is not a chapter about survival in general, but a chapter that covers the role of fires in relation to survival. "To survive" means to "stay alive." A fire has, many times, and may again in the future determine whether or not someone spending an unexpected night or two out lives or dies. If you've read the previous chapters, and even if you haven't, you might remember that fires give warmth, dry clothes, provide a way to signal for help, allow primitive tool-making, disinfect water, and cook food. The heat of a fire means that if you're stuck out there a long time, you'll need to eat fewer calories to keep on living. A fire can also give you a psychological kick in the pants—it can help you want to stay alive. The act of building a fire is an affirmative action, a way of saying to yourself that you will survive.

After stating all of that, here is another important point: a fire is not mandatory to survival, even in extremes of cold and wet. If you are dressed appropriately, and if you know how to take care of yourself outdoors in general, you can survive without a fire. Peoples native to the Arctic region, for instance, do it all the time. Here are three things to consider: 1) If you have adequate clothing, your shelter can be less than ideal; 2) If you have less than adequate clothing, you'll need a splendid shelter; 3) If you have poor clothing and no way to construct a great shelter, you'll probably need a fire. But you need to conserve and preserve your energy, your life force—so if you decide to build a fire, consider whether or not the energy required to get it going and keep it going will be worth the effort.

If you need or just want a fire in a survival situation, you have to, of course, be able to build one. Since the goal is to stay alive, you don't want to depend on primitive fire-making skills, even though you may be competent in those skills (SEE CHAPTER 3). There is wisdom in the old outdoor adage: Always carry two sure methods—such as waterproofed matches **and** a lighter—of applying heat to tinder. The addition of a small candle to your pack gives you excellent fire starting capability. If you're headed way out, exposing yourself intentionally to the possibility of getting stranded, you would be wise to pack as well a commercial fire starter, a chemical or other product that ignites easily and burns hotly (SEE CHAPTER 3).

When you build a fire in extreme circumstances, because of the extreme circumstances, you need—as always, but more so now—to have safety as a first priority. The guidelines you already knew or learned from this book about how to make a safe fire must be followed. Your energy cannot be wasted treating burned flesh, putting out unwanted flames, or, even worse, fleeing from a raging wildfire.

FIRE TO STAY WARM

You can survive for days without water, weeks without food, but sometimes only hours without maintaining the core heat in your body. If you're cold and wet, you need to get warm and dry—and a fire can be a quick route to both. And once you're warm and dry, a fire can help you stay warm and dry.

Choose a site for your survival fire that's dry and out of the wind. You don't want to waste fuel and heat. Dampness sucks up heat, and wind swirls it away while causing your precious fuel to burn far too swiftly. Wind also greatly increases the risk your fire will spread to unwanted places (SEE CHAPTER 8). If there are no natural windbreaks, build one out of

> **A SURVIVAL HIERARCHY:**
> 1. *Don't panic. Stop and think. Plan to survive.*
> 2. *Dress appropriately— your first line of defense against the loss of body heat.*
> 3. *Find shelter, to further conserve body heat.*
> 4. *Find water. Three days without water is a threat to life.*
> 5. *Build a fire.*

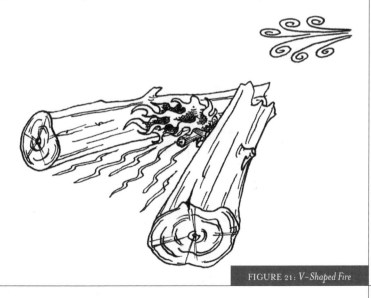

FIGURE 21: *V-Shaped Fire*

logs and/or rocks. Logs may be stacked or, if they're large enough, two can be set to form a V with the fire in the crotch of the V. Remember, if you use rocks, to use dry rocks. Rocks taken from water or swampy ground can explode in the heat of a fire. In the absence of logs or rocks, you can make a serviceable wall by stacking up branches. If you can dig without undue effort, you can also build a windbreak out of dirt.

If you've built a wind-breaking wall of logs, rocks, or branches, they will also serve as a reflector of the fire's heat. You'd never do this in another situation, but you may also build your fire against the base of a large rock, the rock serving as a reflector, or against the base of a rocky cliff for the same reason. The point of the fire reflector is to direct more of the heat toward you. Otherwise a huge percentage of the heat you create, heat that could be warming you, will uselessly warm the night. If you can set up a

Reflecting wall of stacked logs

Plastic shelter

FIGURE 22: *Fire Reflected into a Shelter*

shelter (a sheet of plastic, for instance) or build a shelter from what you can find (such as branches and leaves) or find a shelter (say, underneath a partially fallen tree), your shelter should be situated on the opposite side of the fire from the reflector. The reflected heat should warm you and your shelter. If you cannot construct a shelter, place yourself between the fire and the reflector. Once the reflector is warmed by the heat, you'll have a heat source behind you as well as in front.

On a snow-bound winter day, when a fire may be most desirable, it will also be, usually, the most difficult conditions in which to build one. Winter fires are addressed in Chapter 3, but in a survival situation you may choose to break some of the rules. You may, for instance, burn small dead limbs broken from trees and even an occasional piece of green wood as a signal.

Despite common belief to the contrary, your survival fire should not be big. Keep it small, the heat concentrated and reflected. Being close to a small fire keeps you just as warm as situating yourself farther from a large one—and a small fire conserves your fuel. A small fire only requires small pieces of fuel, a bonus since gathering large amounts of fuel demands more energy, and you want to conserve your energy, a point I make as much as possible. There is an old saying worth remembering: "A small fire keeps you warm with its heat, a large fire keeps you warm running for firewood." A small fire also reduces the chances you'll burn something you don't want to burn, such as your shelter or the forest.

When it's time for sleep, bank your fire well (SEE CHAPTER 3). It's much more energy efficient to add kindling to hot coals than to start a new fire. In a survival situation, after scraping the hot coals into a mound, place large logs on the coals. Hot coals under large logs may maintain enough heat to ignite tinder for 24 hours or more.

Just a reminder: you will not need a reflector fire for warmth if you're stranded with a fine sleeping bag and your tent.

FIRE TO DRY OUT THE WET

Even if you don't immediately need a fire for warmth, you will find one extremely useful to dry out wet and damp clothing. Evaporation, the vaporization of moisture from your skin, draws off an enormous amount of body heat. Proper outdoor clothing—several layers of synthetic material—allows you to retain a large amount of your personal heat even while wearing wet clothes. But you'll be more comfortable and warmer in dry clothing. You want dampness out of your clothing as soon as you can safely get it out.

If you have nothing else to wear, allow your clothing to dry on your body as you sit near the fire. Open your clothing as much as possible to get the drying heat to inner layers. This will work, and it may be the best method if it's really cold and/or you're not feeling the heat loss from wet clothing too tremendously. If you can safely remove layers, they'll dry faster if hung near the fire. You may choose to remove a layer, allow it to dry near the fire, then put it back on after removing another layer to hang near the heat.

The mistake you don't want to make is being in a hurry. Drying is a time-intensive process, haste makes waste, and the waste may be represented by a melted polypropylene shirt or singed jacket. Do not hang clothing directly over the flames. It's too hot. You'll get the best results if you can build a rack of sticks to support the clothing near the side of the fire. And do not leave your clothing unattended. Check it every few minutes with your hand. If the clothing feels warm, that's good. If it feels hot, that's bad. Move hot items farther from the heat.

FIRE TO DISINFECT WATER AND COOK

Dehydration, the loss of normal fluid volume in your body, is a killer. Mild dehydration kills your ability to think straight, your ability to reason. Your energy is killed by further dehydration, and finally, in severe cases, it will kill you. To survive beyond a few days, you must find water. For that

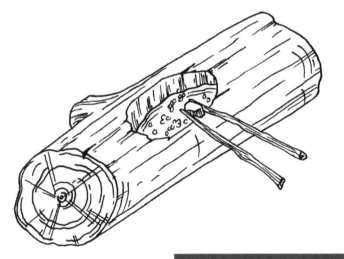

FIGURE 23: *Boiling Water with Red Hot Rocks*

reason, attempt to find a site for your shelter and/or your fire near a source of water.

In all cases, water will be safer to drink if it's brought first to a boil. It doesn't have to boil for several minutes to be safe. It only has to reach the boiling point. Water can be brought to the boiling point in any metal container placed over a flame or in hot coals.

If you only have nonmetal containers, water can be boiled by heating up rocks until they're red hot and placing them in the container with water. As a rule of thumb, two baseball-sized rocks, red hot, will bring about a gallon of water to the boiling point. Without a container of any sort, you can make one by hollowing out a bowl-shaped depression in a log.

In case you have some food you want to cook, red-hot rocks in a container of water can maintain heat long enough for strips of meat or vegetables to cook. Use one or two rocks to start, replacing them with new hot rocks when the first ones cool off. With a fire, you have several other cooking methods available, and you can read about them in Chapter 7.

FIRE TO SIGNAL

If you want someone to find you and rescue you from a potentially deadly situation, you want to make yourself as visible as possible—and fires offer a way to greatly increase your chances of being noticed. Fires in areas where there are not supposed to be fires often bring rangers or other land managers to the scene. They may be unhappy about the illegal fire, you may be fined, but you'll be alive to pay the fine.

Since you want to make your signal fires as visible as possible, build them in a clearing. Since you want the fires to be visible in all directions, building them in a clearing on a ridge would be even better. Without a clearing, look for an area of the forest where the trees are widely spaced. Any trees, however, will dissipate light and smoke, and make you more difficult to spot.

Contrast is the key to effective signaling. Bright fires at night contrast with the darkness. Green and other damp wood, green leaves, moss, ferns, and water sprinkled on a fire create a lot of white smoke, and smoky fires by day contrast with dark soil and green vegetation. If the smoke rises high enough, it will contrast with the blue sky. The hotter the fire, the higher the smoke will rise. On a clear, calm day, searchers have reported seeing smoke from a fire 50 miles away. White smoke, of course, provides little contrast with snow-covered ground. Although they might not be available, oil-soaked rags, rubber, and plastic make dark smoke. Experiment with the materials you have at hand, and use the fuel that makes the darkest smoke

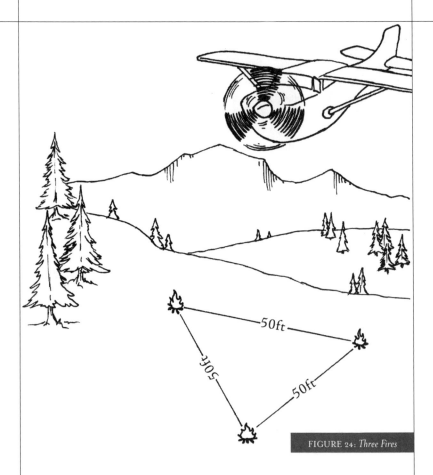

FIGURE 24: *Three Fires*

as a contrast with snow—but don't burn something you might need later if your smoke isn't seen.

If someone knows your trip plans, including when to expect you back, you can be pretty sure someone is searching for you, and a lone fire is often enough. But three of anything is a universal signal for help, and three fires would be better than one. Trained searchers look for three fires set in an equilateral triangle or spaced out equally apart in a straight line. If the fires are set about 50 to 100 feet apart, experts agree you have maximized your chances of having them seen.

If firewood is in short supply, your best bet is to get the fires ready for a match but don't light them until you hear an airplane. Although there is wisdom in the previous sentence, frantically trying to get signal fires going quickly may prove a ferociously frustrating experience. But it's better than burning your fuel with little hope of being spotted. If firewood is abundant, keep the fires small and a large supply of dry fuel ready to throw on the coals with a moment's notice.

Now relax as much as possible. You have done what you can, and you will live to see another day.

CHAPTER 7

THE TASTE
of
FIRE

"*Much of the success of a camping trip, as well as a great deal of pleasure, is going to depend on your having the right kind of fires. This does not mean, certainly, that campfires should be built in just one way. It all depends upon where you are, what you have, and whether your most pressing needs at the moment are for warmth, light, or nourishment.*"

BRADFORD ANGIER AND COLONEL TOWNSEND WHELEN, 1958

BACK IN THE OLD DAYS, when I began my career as an outdoor educator, if we cooked we cooked on a fire. We didn't carry a backpacking stove. Our pots and pans were as black as a moonless midnight and aromatic with pitch and soot. We taught our students how to cook on fires. We taught them to make fires, maintain fires, kill fires, and disguise the fact that they had used fires. Despite our efforts to the contrary, however, we left plenty of scars on the land. Because it's important, we now teach people how to live well outdoors without a fire. The only constant, said someone wise, is change.

But when it's acceptable today, cooking on an open fire, rapidly becoming a lost art, can add a heaping measure of fun, wonder, dietary ash, and the taste of smoke to your next outdoor trip. If you've ever, and you most likely have, roasted a marshmallow over a bed of coals, perhaps even a hot dog, and you know something of what I'm talking about. But hot dogs are difficult to ruin, even over open flames, while a meal that reaches at least a little bit toward culinary excellence requires more than a stick and a bun. What you'll find in this chapter is a pot-full of thoughts on campfire cooking, tips on several methods, and a few recipes that go along with the methods. But first let's take a look at the impact of a cooking fire.

THE CAMP KITCHEN: AN ENVIRONMENTAL VIEWPOINT

In addition to the impact of your fire already discussed (SEE CHAPTER 5), you increase the chances you'll leave a mess behind any time you cook outdoors. There's the trash, but there's also the food scraps that tempt wildlife and lead to contamination of the environment. Build your cooking fire at least 200 feet (about 70 adult paces) away from water sources to prevent contamination of the water. Do your food prep on a cloth or sheet of plastic to catch the crumbs. They can be shaken off the cloth into your garbage bag and packed out. A few crumbs may also be dumped in the fire. Plan all your meals thoughtfully, especially in relation to how much you cook. Cook only as much as you can eat. Leftovers, in most cases, are unsavory and unburnable—as well as wasteful. Gather all your trash carefully, burning the paper and packing out the unburnable material.

In a way, a campfire cook is no better than the fire he or she builds out of the remnants of what was once a tree. There's a lot about sizes and shapes of campfires in Chapter 3, but whatever the shape, you'll want to keep your blaze, as almost always, small. You don't need a lot of heat, and the heat you make needs to be concentrated under and/or around the pot, pan, or slab of meat. Most meals should actually be cooked over coals,

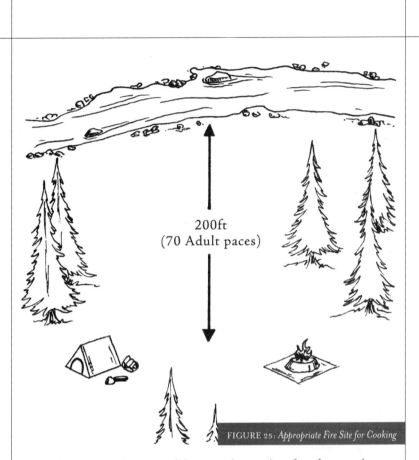

200ft
(70 Adult paces)

FIGURE 25: *Appropriate Fire Site for Cooking*

since flames create far too much heat—unless you're a fan of raw steak seared black on the outside or noodles baked to the floor of the pot. An exception to the general rule of coals for cooking might be boiling water for soup, pasta, or coffee. Water will boil faster when a pot is suspended over flames (**SEE BELOW**), but water will boil, even if you watch the pot, on a heap of hot coals. And, to prevent adding injury to insult, a roaring blaze makes it mighty hard on the chef.

Gather enough firewood to prevent a trip for more in the middle of preparation of the food. The unused wood will, remember, be scattered back into the forest. Since you're after the best coals possible, look for the hardest wood you can find (**SEE CHAPTER 4**). And the wood needs to be as dry as possible. The damper the wood, the more smoke and the less cleanly the wood burns. When the wood has burned down to coals a couple of inches thick, you're usually ready to cook. Another method I use to test coals requires exposing my naked hand to the heat: when the coals are about the right temperature, I can hold my hand six to eight inches over them for six to eight seconds. You'll need to check the coals now and then, and add more pieces of small wood if the temperature drops too low. Don't forget that food cooking over a fire, small or large, should never be left alone. Fire can turn what would have been a tasty meal into a burned, crusty mess in a very short time.

POT AND PAN COOKING

Most campfire cooks prepare meals in pots and pans, the same approach to a feast you use when the food will cook over a backpacking stove. For pot or pan cooking, the fire or bed of coals, on most days, really needs to be no larger than the bottom of the pot or pan you'll cook in. The ubiquitous backpacking banquets that require no more than boiling water added to a pouch of dried stuff can be ruined, in my opinion, with an improper pot. A proper pot has a snug fitting lid. Without the lid the water, then the food, soon acquires a distinctive smoky taste that's fine with a hot dog but disgusting in oatmeal or freeze-dried pasta primavera. A snug lid also means your water will boil faster. A sturdy pot—I prefer stainless steel or titanium—can be placed directly on a bed of coals, but suspending the pot over the coals offers a couple of advantages, including ease of removal from the heat and, as mentioned earlier, faster boiling. A simple method is to place a pot on two small logs placed across the coals, separated just enough to allow heat to rise between the logs. This method, unfortunately, leaves you with two fire-scarred logs that must be burned down to ash—otherwise you leave an ugly reminder of your visit. You may also balance pots and pans on two or three spaced rocks, but this method leaves you with soot-blackened rocks that may have to be hidden. A more sophisticated method is to prop a strong stick over the coals and hang the pot by its handle from the stick. You need to plan ahead to use this method since many pots have no handles. With a hanging pot, you can pile the coals up close for a raging boil or spread them out underneath for a slower boil. With a hanging pot, you can also suddenly find your dinner in the coals—so make sure the strong stick is very strong and placed very securely. Be warned: the handle of the pot will heat up soon after the pot. You want to wear durable gloves, padded kitchen mittens, and/or use strong potgrips to remove the pot from the fire.

If your meal can be prepared in a frying pan, a pan with a long metal handle makes cooking much easier. Even with a long handle, wearing durable gloves is a good idea. The pan, as with the pot, can be placed directly on the coals or suspended over the heat between two logs. Timid about these balancing acts? You can always pack in a collapsible campfire grill that stands over the coals on legs of its own or rests on two logs or rocks. A grill greatly reduces the chance you'll have to deal with partially burned logs of larger wood. Grilling, by the way, is my favorite way to cook meat over a fire. The best way to control the heat in the pan, with or without a grill, is by periodically lifting it above the fire—a little lift equals a small reduction in heat, a big lift equals a big reduction.

When frying most food you'll need grease. Butter serves as a superior grease because its flavor is superb. On the other hand, it demands the greatest attention due to a low smoking point. Margarine and oil burn less easily but are not as tasty. Whatever you use for frying, keep an eye constantly open for smoking, an indication that the grease is far too hot. Lift the pan high enough above the coals to stop the smoking while your pancake, eggs, fish, or steak fries without scorching. Since the way you cook with pots and pans over a fire differs from stovetop cooking only in how you manage the heat, you can cook the same foods in the woods that you cook at home.

FIGURE 26: *Pot Suspended over Fire*

DUTCH OVEN COOKING

A Dutch oven is the oldest metal-utensil method of cooking on a fire, and certainly the most versatile. It does, however, involve more firewood than pot-and-pan cooking. Inside a Dutch oven you can shallow fry, deep fry, roast, bake, poach, or stew, in addition to boil. A well-made Dutch oven has a strong handle, allowing you to suspend it over open flames or coals. But you'll most often set one directly in coals, or even bury one deeply in coals. Made of cast iron or thick aluminum, a Dutch oven tends to be heavy, often real heavy. I've had great success using, instead, the much lighter Banks Fry-Bake Pan with its tight-fitting lid. You can't hang it over a fire, but you will find it extremely versatile and great for baking with coals.

Use a Dutch oven the same as a pot or frying pan for boiling or frying. If you're going to roast, bake, or stew, place the Dutch oven directly in the coals, bank the coals around the oven, and pile coals on top of the oven, being sure to seat the lid well first. You can tell you'll need quite a few coals. The coals on top will need the addition of twigs from time to time to keep enough heat on all sides of the cooking food. When baking, be sure to grease the inside of the oven well to

FIGURE 27: *Grill Set Over Coals*

Flip-Baked Bread

2 cups flour
1/4 cup dry milk
4 teaspoons baking powder
1/4 cup cooking oil
pinch of salt
1-1/4 to 1-1/2 cups of water

Mix the dry ingredients well. Slowly add the water, mixing it in until your dough has the consistency of thick mud. It should slide off your spoon, but it shouldn't be in a hurry. Smear your frying pan well with cooking oil. (You can use butter, but you have to be very careful about the heat.) Press the dough gently into the pan, and place the pan over the coals. When the edges get sort of brown, flip the dough carefully over and continue cooking until both sides are toasty and the middle is not gooey. Time per side depends on the thickness of the dough and the heat of the fire. When it's well done, the bread will have a hollow sound when you thump it with a flicked finger. You can vary this recipe by substituting a cup of cornmeal for a cup of flour and end up with flip-baked cornbread. Or you can throw a half cup of sugar into the dry ingredients, maybe a handful of raisins, and end up with dessert.

Frypan Oat Cakes

2-1/4 cups white flour *1 cup wheat flour* *3/4 cup oatmeal* *1 teaspoon salt* *1/2 cup sugar* *2 teaspoons baking powder* *2 tablespoons dry milk* *1 teaspoon cinnamon* *1/2 cup cooking oil* *about 1 cup water*	Mix the oil, sugar, dry milk, and water in a pot and bring the mixture to a boil. Stir until sugar is dissolved and remove from heat. Add the rest of the dry ingredients to the sugary milk mixture, and stir until all ingredients are moist. You'll now have dough from which you can pinch off balls that you shape into round cakes. Press the round cakes gently into a well-greased frying pan and flip-bake as described in Flip-Baked Bread (SEE PAGE 70). Make more than you can eat of these. They'll last quite a while in your pack.

prevent sticking of the dough. You can, for instance, pack in a box of commercially prepared cake mix, and bake up a sumptuous dessert in a Dutch over. If you're following a recipe, a Dutch oven typically requires approximately the same amount of time to roast, bake, or stew as in your oven at home—that is if you've made an appropriate bed of coals first.

FOIL COOKING

You've probably pulled enough aluminum foil out of the ashes of old campfires to know from experience that foil won't burn. That can work in your favor if you choose the simple campfire cooking method of placing foil-wrapped food directly in the coals, a technique that requires the same amount or even less wood than pot cooking. Many foods (such as meat, potatoes, onions, carrots, squash, and apples) can be cooked in aluminum foil in the coals of a campfire. Onions are especially difficult to ruin. If the taste of onion will benefit the meal, a layer of onions on the bottom will enhance flavor, even if the onions burn. Whatever you cook, begin by rubbing plenty of butter on the inside of the foil to prevent sticking.

Predictors of success also include 1) using heavy-duty foil, and 2) using a large enough piece of foil, one that allows you to seal the food tightly inside. You need to be able to double-fold the ends of the foil. After the food is placed on the foil, flatten the edges of the foil and fold the edges over about three-quarter of an inch. Then fold the edge a second time.

Before placing the foil-wrapped food in the coals, let the coals die down more than you would when using other methods. Too much heat can rapidly burn your meal. Don't worry if the coals have turned a disconcerting grayish-white with the appearance of a lack of heat. White

FIGURE 28: *Dutch Oven Buried in Coals*

ash will hold the heat of the coals underneath for an adequate amount of time to cook dinner. Snuggle the foil-wrapped package in the coals and enjoy another cup of coffee or hot chocolate while the food cooks. But don't leave the food in the heat any longer than necessary. Not only will the food burn, but the foil will begin to fall apart, making it more difficult to make sure you've removed it completely from the coals in order to pack out every scrap. When you think the coals have done their job, fish out a package and press it with a gloved hand. A nice squishy feel usually means the cooking has gone long enough. Some experimentation is required for the novice. If you unwrap the food and find it not yet completely cooked to your satisfaction, you can return it to the coals for more cooking.

STICK COOKING

Requiring another piece of the forest, but not a huge one, no open fire method is simpler, in terms of utensils, than stick cooking. You'll need a stick about half an inch thick and, say, four feet long—or, if you've planned

Dutch Oven Rice

2 large onions
bacon, several strips
1 cup quick-cooking rice
grated cheese
pinch of salt
1 large tomato
butter

Chop the onions and bacon as the Dutch oven heats in the coals. Stir-fry the onions and bacon (with a dab of butter for extra flavor) for a few minutes. Add 2 cups of hot water to the oven with the cup of rice—and for Pete's sake don't stir the rice. Place the lid securely on the oven. While the rice cooks, cut up the tomato. When the rice is cooked, remove the oven from the heat, mix with the tomato and salt, and sprinkle the grated cheese on top.

ahead, carry a coat hanger with you to unbend into a "stick." A wooden stick will require sharpening on one end. If the bark is still on the stick, I leave it in most cases, but I do wash the cooking end, rubbing off the loose bark and debris. A little bark keeps food from rotating on the stick when you turn it over the coals, a problem that may leave you frustrated with a half-cooked dinner. If you've chosen a coat hanger, remember the entire length of metal may grow hot before dinner is ready and wearing gloves to handle the metal can add to your enjoyment. For those deeply committed to stick cooking on a coat hanger, you can make a handle by splitting a short piece of wood, slipping one end of the hanger into the split, and tying the split wood securely closed.

You're somewhat limited in what you can stick cook: meat, or vegetables cut small but not so small they fall apart when you skewer the pieces, or some type of batter you can wrap around the stick. Fish can be spitted through the mouth and down into the intestinal cavity. Red meat should be cut no more than an inch thick and pulled onto the spit through pre-sliced holes. You can hold the skewered food over the coals, if you're patient, or prop one end over a rock or log with the other end held down by a second rock or log. Slow cooking creates a tastier meal, so don't suspend the food too close to the coals. If you have too much heat, the outside chars while the inside stays raw. Rotate the stick when the surface of the food facing the heat appears done. With several variables at play, the best way to know the food is cooked to your taste is by tasting.

YIPPEE-KI-YAY COWBOY COFFEE:

In addition to a fire, all you need is an old pot, the older the better, and lots of ground coffee beans. For every cup of water in the pot, approximately, put in a heaping tablespoon of coffee, approximately. Always throw in a little extra coffee . . . for the pot. Put the pot over the heat, and watch it impatiently. You're watching to make sure it doesn't boil. When coffee boils it starts to get bitter. Just as the black water starts to move around, take the pot off the fire and cover it, and wait a few minutes for the grounds to settle. Pour off a steaming cup while unsuccessfully trying to keep all the grounds in the pot. Whilke drinking, spit out the grounds that work their way into your mouth. This is a necessary and treasured aspect of cowboy coffee. If you choke a little on the first and last swallow, it's probably just right.

Hamburger-in-Foil	
1/2 pound hamburger 1 carrot 1 small potato 1 small onion butter	Cut up the vegetables. Make the hamburger into a patty. Smear some butter on the foil and place some of the vegetables on the foil, then the patty, then the rest of the vegetables. Securely close the foil and snuggle the package into the coals. Cook about 12 minutes, roll the foil package over, and cook another 12 minutes. Take care when you do the rolling over. You don't want to tear the foil or burn your hand. To save time, you can prepare this foil dinner before leaving home, and carry it in a plastic bag in case juice leaks out. Don't be afraid to add other foods you like to the recipe, such as green pepper, tomato, or pineapple.

SPIT COOKING

When you want to cook something large, something that doesn't skewer well when cut into small pieces, such a chicken or a small furry mammal (with fur removed), you'll do better by spit cooking, a glorified method

Potato-in-Foil	
1 large baking potato 1 large onion butter	Slice the potato almost all the way through in a half dozen or so places. Make sure you don't slice it all the way through. Cut the onion into slices, and place a slice of onion in each cut in the potato. Fold the whole thing securely in butter-smeared foil. Place in it coals for about 45 minutes. Enjoy some cheese and crackers, or conversation, or the sunset. When you think the potato is done, stick a fork through the foil. If the potato is done, the fork will slip out without lifting the potato. For a taste bonus, sprinkle on some grated cheese, or some salt and pepper, or both, after unwrapping the spud.

of stick cooking. In this case, the skewered meat is held over the coals by propping up both ends of the stick. A popular method of suspension is to bury forked sticks in the ground on both sides of the fire, but you can also stack rocks on both sides of the fire and lay the spit across the top of the stacks. A spit allows you to easily rotate your dinner over the coals, and rotate you should every three or four minutes.

To skewer an animal on the spit, run a sharp stick from head to tail along the underside of the backbone. Many woods will add an unpleasant taste to the meat, but searing the stick in the heat of the fire first will eliminate most of the taste of wood. Searing the meat first, too, will seal in the juices, making your repast less dry and more tasty.

Be prepared for a long wait. Spit cooking takes a lot of time. You can speed up the process with an old mountain-man technique. Slice off the outer layer of meat after it has cooked, and eat it while the next layer cooks. You never get the really tender inner meat which long, slow cooking produces, but you get to eat sooner.

FIGURE 29: *Spit Cooking*

ROCK COOKING

Here's one from the really old days. Although it can be interesting to experiment with several ways to cook with hot rocks, I wouldn't use any of them again unless I was desperate. Not only will you leave ugly, blackened rocks behind, an eyesore for the next hiker, but the food sometimes tastes like rock. The best cooking rock is large, flat, and no more than about two inches thick. The thinner the rock the better. You can use a rock that's rounded on one side, flat on the other, but it's more tedious. Place the rock in hot coals or suspend the rock, balanced on other rocks, over the coals. Choose a dry rock, not one from a creek, which could have collected enough water to explode when the temperature rises high, ruining dinner. Give yourself plenty of time to let the rock heat up, then turn it over but leave it over the heat, blow off as much of the ash as you can, and cook on the hot side. This is sort of a primitive stir-fry method, not lending itself well to foods that take a long

Stick Bread

1 cup all-purpose flour
1 teaspoon double-
acting baking powder
pinch of salt
1 tablespoon butter or
cooking oil
a little water

Few campfire foods have as much appeal and offer as much satisfaction as fresh bread. This recipe is for the basic bannock of yesteryear, and it can be cooked when the nearest utensil is dozens of miles away. Don't mix the ingredients until you've prepared the fire and the stick. In fact, if you don't want to mix the ingredients at all, carry Bisquick. This stick should be peeled down to bare wood—no bark. Thoroughly mix the flour, baking powder, and salt. Option: You can add powdered milk, just a tablespoon or two, for more nutrition. Soften the butter near the heat, then mix it well with the dry ingredients. Add just enough water to make a firm dough. Too much or too little water, and the dough won't stick to the stick, which it must. If the water is really cold, let it warm a bit by the fire first. Warm water encourages the baking powder to do its job of fluffing up the dough when it cooks. Hint: It's easier to add a little more water than a little more flour to reach the right consistency. When you can toss the dough ball easily from hand to hand, it's probably ready. Roll it out in your hand until it's long and slim. Then wrap it around the stick and bake it over the coals. When it's golden brown on the outside, it's usually ready. For a dessert option, add dried fruit, sugar, cinnamon, etc., to the dry mix, then add water and bake.

time to fry and not for someone who can't tolerate a substantial sprinkling of ash in dinner. Successful rock cooking, like many methods of campfire cooking, includes plenty of practice and a smidgen of good luck.

You can also boil water, and the food in the pot with the water, by placing red-hot rocks in the container with the water. This is a tedious method of cooking, typically used only in extreme situations (SEE CHAPTER 6).

CAMP KITCHEN CLEAN-UP

After eating, if you haven't caught and/or picked up very last crumb and tossed them into the fire, do it now. Remember: don't try to burn leftovers. It doesn't work. Pack them out. And never bury leftovers. Animals will dig them up.

If you've used pots or pans, clean them right away. The longer you wait, the more aggressively food sticks to the cooking surface. A little thinking ahead will go a long way here. Put a pot of water over the coals while you're enjoying dinner. With hot water and a scrubbing sponge you don't need soap—and soap, even biodegradable soap, leaves pollution behind. With hot water in the pots, bowls, cups, or whatever you've used, simply scrub them clean.

Do not toss the "gray water," the water filled with food scraps, into the forest. Strain the dirty water through a small strainer, a coffee filter, or even a bandanna, and pack out the food scraps in your garbage bag. If you're not prepared to strain, and even if you are, you can always drink the gray water. Yes, it's safe, it reduces the weight in your garbage bag, and your body probably needs more hydration. Throw in a flavored drink mix, and it might even taste okay as you sip quietly (and chew) while watching the fire die.

S'MORES:

The most famous stick-prepped snack of all time, s'mores, got their name from the claim that once you eat one you'll want "some more." The original s'more is made of Graham crackers, milk chocolate, and marshmallows. Break the Graham cracker in half and lay a chunk of chocolate on one half. Roast a marshmallow or two until you've got a mass of thoroughly hot sugar. Pull the marshmallow off the stick by placing in on the chocolate and smashing the second half of the cracker against it—and gently removing the stick. Give the resulting cookie a minute or two so the chocolate can melt. But don't be constrained by the original recipe. Use your imagination. A rice cake instead of a Graham cracker, for instance, yields a totally delicious snack—and it's bigger!

CHAPTER 8

WILD
FIRE

"Have you ever seen a forest fire? It is terrible. Thousands of acres are destroyed, and
many a time men and women and children have been cut off by a tornado of
flame and burned alive. The person whose carelessness starts such a
holocaust is worse than a fool—he is a criminal, and a disgrace
to the good earth he treads."

HORACE KEPHART, 1917

IN AUGUST OF 1977, before it was officially declared
"out," the Marble Cone Fire burned approximately 178,000 acres of
chaparral and mixed forestland. Only two forest fires in the known history
of California were more destructive. By day the sun was a bleary, red bulb
barely visible through the dense smoke. By night the fierce red glow of
flame could be seen for many miles in every direction, made ghostly and
unreal by the smoky haze. Firefighters were called in from around the na-
tion. It was a war. "Troops" wearing no-burn uniforms, mostly yellow and
green, sweating under hard helmets, armed with shovels and half-ax/half-
hoe pulaskis, manned the fire lines. Planes flew low, dropping great, sweep-
ing, liquid bombs of pink fire retardant. Helicopters scooped up huge
buckets of the Pacific Ocean, and dumped them on the flames. Despite the
inferno, despite several firefighter entrapments, there were zero human fatalities. I'm personally happy to be able to report no loss of human life—I
had been one of the entrapped.

Wildland fires—highly destructive wildfires on land that is unculti-
vated or unfit for cultivation—have been a part of the natural history of
Earth since long before any humans were around to watch them or run
away from them. Only relatively recently in human history have we chosen
to make a stand against wildland fires and attempt to suppress them (SEE
BELOW). From the study of such fires, experts now divide them into three
classes: ground, surface, and crown. Ground fires burn grass and other
low-lying vegetation. Surface fires burn grass, low-lying vegetation, and
the trunks of trees. Crown fires climb all the way up trees, reaching their
crowns (tops), and then rage across the top of the forest. Crown fires are
the most destructive—and the most dangerous.

"Only you can prevent forest fires," says Smoky the Bear, but, will all
due respect, Smoky isn't technically correct. Yes, outrageous and massively
ruinous wildfires—fires around the world—are often started by human
activity, sometimes by careless hikers or campers, sometimes
by arsonists. But lightning has been and will persist as the primary
non-human igniter of destructive flames, as was the case in the Marble
Cone Fire. In the United States, an average of 5 million acres burn wildly
every year. Once fully involved, wildfire feeds itself, promotes itself, ensures
its own survival (SEE CHAPTER 2). It spreads with incredible speed.
Wildfire spreads have been clocked at 14.3 miles per hour, and at their
fierce height can toss burning material for miles around. Three factors
determine how fast and how far a wildfire spreads—fuel, weather, and
topography.

FUEL

The amount of burnable stuff available to feed a wildfire—the living and standing dead trees, the downed timber, the brush, and grass—is known as the fuel load. Generally speaking, a wildfire burns hotter, and therefore spreads faster, with a large fuel load. But other characteristics of fuel come into play.

The moisture content of the fuel, as always, determines how fast it will reach ignition temperature. The drier the fuel, the faster the fire spreads. Fuel with a large surface area compared to its volume, twigs for instance, ignite much faster than big chunks of wood—so fuel size also contributes to how fast a wildfire spreads. Finally, the arrangement of the fuel relates to the spread of fire. When fuels are spaced out, they hold their moisture less aggressively and more oxygen can get to the flames. Fires spread more rapidly when spaces separate fuels than when fuels are packed tightly together. All of these factors come into play when a fuel load is evaluated.

WEATHER

The state of the atmosphere in relation to its temperature, moisture, and movement are critical factors in the spread of wildfire. When the air is hot, fuels are warmer and they ignite quicker and burn faster. This fact explains why wildfires tend to burn more intensely in the afternoon, when air temperatures reach their peaks. When the air is moist, due to humidity and/or precipitation, fuels are, naturally, moister and more difficult to ignite. To put it another way: warm, dry air promotes wildfire, and cold, moist air reduces the risk of wildfire.

URBAN WILDFIRES

Destructive, uncontrollable wildfires are not limited to forests. Urban wildfires are almost daily occurrences, giving rise to local fire departments all around the world and powerful films such as Ladder 49. *The most famous wildfires have undoubtedly been urban. For instance:*

On September 2, 1666, fire escaped from a bakery in London. Five days later an area 1.5 miles by 0.5 miles, essentially the city, lay in ashes. An estimated 13,200 homes were destroyed—plus 87 churches. The Great Fire of London, remarkably, caused only six known human fatalities.

On October 8, 1871, a barn in Chicago erupted in flame. Legend blames Mrs. O'Leary's cow for kicking over a kerosene lamp. Two days later, after the fire spread ferociously, 300 Chicagoans were dead, and 90,000 were homeless. The Great Chicago Fire sputtered out in a downpour of rain.

But wind impacts wildfire more than all other weather conditions. Wind dries fuel, keeps the flames supplied with oxygen, and urges fire to move across the terrain. The faster the wind speed, the faster the fire spreads. Raging wildfires create their own wind, sometimes called fire whirls. Like a tornado, hot air spirals upward with the tumultuous rising of the fire's heat. Wind created by huge wildfires can be 10 times faster than the ambient wind blowing of its own accord. Wildfire-generated wind lifts flames into the tops of the trees, causing crown fires. If these "tornados" tilt from vertical to horizontal, as they sometimes do, the fire not only speeds up but also can, as mentioned earlier, throw burning debris over great distances.

TOPOGRAPHY

Although fuel and weather will vary, the shape of the terrain remains unchanged, yet topography contributes to the spread, or the early death, of a wildfire. The most critical aspect of topography is its slope. Fire spreads uphill much faster than it spreads downhill—with a possible exception in the case of a powerful, and unusual, downhill wind. Heat rises, so uphill fuel dries and heats faster. The steeper the slope, the more aggressive the

SOME OF THE UNITED STATES' WORST FOREST FIRES

1871, OCTOBER 8–14	More than 3.8 million acres of Wisconsin burned and more than 1,500 people died in the Great Peshtigo Fire, the worst forest fire in U.S. history.
1894, SEPTEMBER 1	Fire burned more than 160,000 acres of Minnesota, destroying 6 towns and killing over 600 people.
1902, SEPTEMBER	The Yacoult Fire in Washington and Oregon burned 1 million acres and ended the lives of 38 people.
1910, AUGUST 10	Fire destroyed 3 million acres of Idaho and Montana, killing 85 people.
1947, OCTOBER 25–27	Maine lost 205,678 acres, some of it in Acadia National Park, a part of Bar Harbor, and 16 people.
1949, AUGUST 5	In Mann Gulch, Montana, 13 firefighters died in the flames.
1956, NOVEMBER 25	Fire burned 40,000 acres of the Cleveland National Forest in California, killing 11 people.
1970, SEPTEMBER 26	Fire destroyed 175,425 acres of California, including 382 structures in the city of Laguna.

spread of the fire. When the flames reach the top of a ridge or mountain, they lose intensity, and the fire may die.

FIGHTING WILDLAND FIRE

Firefighters, men and women, are highly trained and willing to risk their lives standing before the violent heat and smoke of wildfire. In wildland fire suppression, firefighters (hotshots) typically attack the flames via a ground assault. Others jump from perfectly good airplanes, wearing parachutes, and are called smokejumpers. Smokejumpers are more likely to show up first at remote fire sites where rough terrain delays a ground assault. Hotshots are employed by the U. S. Forest Service (USFS), and smokejumpers by the USFS or the Bureau of Land Management.

In both cases, firefighters may use several methods to fight the fire. When the flames are small, they kill the fire with dirt, water, or chemical fire retardant. Firefighters tend to spend a lot of time building firebreaks, removing all the potential fuel from a strip of land ahead of the fire. Or they may start a backfire, burning the fuel that lies in the path of an oncoming wildfire. Support for the firefighters on the ground often comes from the air in the form of planes and helicopters dropping water or

SOME OF THE UNITED STATES' WORST FOREST FIRES

1988, AUGUST & SEPTEMBER
Over 1.2 million acres of Yellowstone National Park burned.

1994, JULY 2–11
A small fire (approximately 2,000 acres) in South Canyon, Colorado, took the lives of 14 firefighters.

2000, APRIL AND MAY
An estimated 47,000 acres burned in northern New Mexico, and 235 structures were lost.

2000, SPRING & SUMMER
About 7.2 million acres burned nationwide in one of the worst fire seasons in U. S. history—close to twice the 10-year average.

2002, JUNE & JULY
The Hayman Fire, the worst in Colorado's history, destroyed 137,760 acres and 600 structures. At approximately the same time, the Rodeo Fire merged with the Chediski Fire to cause the worst fire in Arizona's history, burning 438,638 acres and more than 400 structures.

2003, OCTOBER
The Cedar Fire, the largest in California's history, destroyed over 200,000 acres. Within the same time period, in a 2-week span, 15 California fires burned 800,000 acres and killed 24 people.

2004, JULY & AUGUST
In the worst fire season ever in Alaska, more than 5 million acres burned.

chemical fire retardant on the blaze. The cost of suppressing wildfire in the United States every year can run to well over a billion dollars per year.

WILDFIRE: ON THE POSITIVE SIDE

Some of the destructiveness of wildfire is obvious—the loss of human life and property; the loss of trees, brush, and habitat for some species of wildlife; the loss of pasturage for livestock; the enormous cost of fire suppression. Wildland fires destroy the beauty of the environment, leaving what is typically thought of as ugly scars on the landscape. Some of the disastrous results are less obvious. With the loss of rooted vegetation on slopes and the weakening of organic material in the soil, for instance, dangerous and destructive erosion problems may occur.

But beneath the destructiveness, wildland fires have a positive side that experts are only just beginning to appreciate. The Wilderness Act of 1964 encouraged those who wanted answers to a couple of questions: 1) Since wilderness areas are places where humans visit without interfering with the natural processes, should we suppress fires in wilderness areas? and 2) since fires are a part of natural history, what purpose do they serve if they're allowed to burn?

Abutting Idaho's Frank Church–River of No Return Wilderness, the Selway-Bitterroot Wilderness of Montana and Idaho is a vast region of designated wildland. In 1972, the U.S. Forest Service began to allow wildfires there to burn without intervention. Their guidelines have been relatively simple. If the fire's source is human, the fire is suppressed. If the fire's source is lightning and it doesn't threaten people or buildings, the fire may be watched but is left alone. Many interesting discoveries related to the benefits of wildfire have been made in the Selway-Bitterroot Wilderness and in a growing number of other areas worldwide where "let-burn" programs have been initiated and studied.

To begin, studies have shown that many fires burn in patches, especially if the fire crowns. Within the boundaries of a fire that involves 100,000 acres, somewhere between 10 and 50 percent may be relatively undamaged. The number of acres that burn can be far less than the number of acres the fires spreads across. In addition, fires do not eliminate life in a burned area. Trees can survive even when their crowns are scorched. Even when crown fires kill large trees, this opens an area of forest to younger trees and trees of different species. Wild animals, too, are able to survive fires, running away or digging deep into burrows.

Simply put, fire is less destructive than once thought and is a relatively cheap land-management tool. Older, and often primitive, cultures have used wildfire for centuries as a way to improve living conditions—most likely noticing the benefits without, at least to some extent, understanding the why. Fires cleared vegetation around campsites and villages, creating a firebreak and the safety of a greater field of vision. Deliberate fires drove game out of dense vegetation where it could be harvested. Burned sites attracted game back into new vegetation. Long ago it was discovered that fires regenerate plants that serve as a food source.

As a modern land-management tool, controlled wildland fires save money that would otherwise be burned in fire suppression. When fire burns underbrush—the small, volatile fuel—the reduction of accumulating fuel tends to reduce the risk of larger future fires, saving money, decreasing injury and illness to firefighters, and enhancing our wildlands. Reaping the benefits of not extinguishing wildfires has led to numerous years of prescribed burns, fires naturally or intentionally started that are allowed to burn under careful scrutiny. The deliberate use of fire in order to prevent later and more intense fires is probably the most common use of fire in modern land management.

Beyond the reduction in fuel—and of greater interest—is that the physical condition of the environment is often ultimately enhanced, sometimes to a large degree, by fire. These changes by fire have a profound effect on the life cycle of the forest. "Fire should not be viewed as a catastrophic event in most situations," writes Robert J. Whelan in his book *The Ecology of Fire*. Wildland ecosystems, to say it another way, not only survive many wildfires, they are made healthier by the fires.

Wildfire reduces the spread of harmful insects and diseases and quickly releases nutrients into the soil from the breakdown of organic matter. Post-fire nutritional surge stimulates fresh plant growth, attracting animals back to burned areas for fresh food. Some species of wildlife find the habitat left by old burns ideal as home, and some species thrive only in old burned areas. There are plants, such as legumes, with seeds that lie dormant in the ground until germinated by the heat of a fire. Some plants wait for more than a century until a big burn creates the conditions they need to sprout and thrive. Some trees—such as lodgepole and jack pine—are serotinous, only able to spread their seeds when fireyburts open their cones. No fires, no baby jacks. Fire promotes and maintains specific species of plants and animals, eliminates undesirable species, and may increase the number of species overall. Carefully controlled, wildfire can even maximize the beneficial runoff of precipitation without erosion. It's a new science, and a lot more study is needed, but it appears that wildfires are necessary to maintain the diversity of life on this planet.

CHAPTER 9

THE BODY
BURNED

"How great a matter a little fire kindleth!"

JAMES 3: 5, THE BIBLE

BURNS TO HUMAN FLESH, even small burns, are

extremely painful. The pain alone makes burns well worth avoiding. But burns can also be permanently disabling, permanently disfiguring, and, if serious, permanently fatal. All you need to get burned, as you know if you've been paying attention to this book, is oxygen, a source of heat, and fuel—and in this case you may be the fuel.

When you realize you—or someone else—have been burned, and that realization tends to come rather quickly, your first action is the most important. You must stop the burning process. A piece of burning wood removed from the campfire does not immediately cease burning—and so, too, with human flesh. Seconds count! No treatment for the burn will be effective until the burning process has stopped. Smother flames, if appropriate, then cool the burn with cool water. Submerge the burned body part in water, or pour water over it, or apply thoroughly wet clothing to the burn. Do not use ice because it's too cold. Keep up the cooling process until the pain is at least temporarily alleviated. If you pull a burned finger out of the water, and it soon starts to hurt again, put it back in the water. There are also several burn treatment materials, commercially manufactured and often sold in outdoor stores, appropriate for application immediately to a burn site, if you've packed some in your first-aid kit. Remove clothing and jewelry from the burn area, but do not try to remove tar or melted plastic (say, that polypropylene shirt) that has stuck to the wound.

ASSESSING THE BURN

After cooling, every aspect of burn treatment depends on your assessment of the depth and extent of the burn, the location of the injury, and the amount of pain being suffered. Even though this assessment may be an estimate, it will be your basis for deciding how the burned person will be managed, whether evacuation to a physician is required, and how urgently an evacuation is required.

EXTENT

The extent of a burn refers to the surface area of a person's body that has been damaged. If the burned area is small, you can estimate the extent of a burn by using the Rule of Palmar Surface: the burned person's palmar surface—not your palmar surface, unless you're the one who got burned—equals about one percent of that person's total body surface area (TBSA). The palmar surface is the surface of the palm and the fingers with the fingers held together.

DEPTH

The depth of a burn refers to how far the damage has extended into the skin. The greater the depth, as you will imagine, the greater the damage. Burn depth is typically ranked as either superficial, partial thickness, or full thickness. A superficial burn has not penetrated the epidermis, the outer layer of skin cells. Partial thickness and full thickness burns have reached down into the dermis, the true skin. Partial thickness burns have reached partially through the skin, and full thickness burns have reached entirely through the skin. The chart below describes degrees of burn depth:

	SUPERFICIAL	PARTIAL THICKNESS	FULL THICKNESS
SKIN LAYER	*Epidermis*	*Epidermis/dermis*	*All layer*
COLOR	*Bright red*	*Red to pale*	*Pale (for scalds), charred (for open flame burns)*
BLISTERS	*None*	*Large, fluid-filled*	*Dry*
PAIN	*Mild to moderate*	*Severe*	*Dull to severe*
HEALING	*Spontaneous; 3–5 days*	*Spontaneous; 1–3 weeks*	*Very slow or never*
SCARRING	*None*	*Moderate*	*Severe*

If the burned area is large, you can use the Rule of Nines: each arm represents approximately nine percent TBSA. Each leg represents 18 percent—the front of the leg 9 percent and the back of the leg 9 percent. The front of the body's trunk represents 18 percent TBSA, and the back of the trunk 18 percent. The head represents nine percent, and the groin one percent. For infants and small children, the head represents a larger percentage and the legs a smaller percentage. This will be mentioned again later: partial thickness burns and full thickness burns that cover more than 15 percent TBSA constitute an immediate threat to life.

LOCATION

Burns to the face—indicated by burned skin, singed facial hair, soot around and/or in the nose and mouth, and/or coughing—may lead to swelling and blockage of the person's airway. The airway may be burned if the person inhaled hot air from the fire. A blocked airway will soon lead to death, and anyone who might have a burned airway needs rapid evacuation.

Burns to areas of special function—hands, feet, armpits, groin— often disable the person permanently, and therefore demand immediate evacuation. Deep circumferential burns, burns entirely around an arm or leg, may swell to the point they cut off circulation beyond the burn, so they demand immediate evacuation as well.

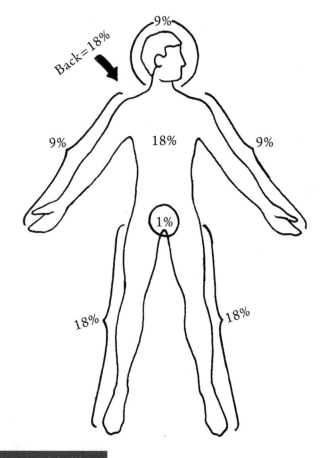

FIGURE 30: *Rule of Nines*

PAIN

In addition to depth and extent, do not underestimate the value of pain as a burn assessment tool. If someone is in a lot of pain, and nothing you do keeps the pain away, that is an indication of the need for prompt and expert medical care.

SPECIFIC BURN MANAGEMENT

Specific burn management is aimed primarily at keeping the wound clean
and reducing pain.

1. Gently wash the burn with slightly warm water and mild soap. Gently
   pat the area dry. If the burns are superficial (see above), the application of a moisturizer is recommended. Remove the skin from blisters
   that have burst, but do not open intact blisters. Gently wipe away obvious dirt and fluid that may leak out of more seriously burned skin.

2. Covering burns reduces pain and slows the loss of body fluid from
   the burn, and both of these are good things to do. Cover burns with
   a thin layer of antibiotic ointment. Silvadene cream, a prescription
   medication, seems to work especially well. You may also cover the
   burn with several products manufactured for that purpose instead
   of ointment, or you may cover the burn with a thin layer of gauze
   impregnated with ointment such as Neosporin or a generic triple-
   antibiotic ointment. If nothing else is available, you can apply dry
   gauze or clean, dry clothing to the burn.

3. When evacuation is imminent (say, within 12 hours or so), leave the
   burn alone from then on. But if evacuation is distant, re-cover the
   burn twice a day by removing old coverings, re-cleaning (and removing the old ointment), and putting on fresh ointment and a clean, dry
   covering. You may have to soak off old dressings with clean, warm
   water.

4. Keep burned extremities (arms and
   legs) elevated above the level of the
   burned person's heart to minimize
   swelling. Swelling retards healing and
   encourages infection.

5. Ibuprofen is probably the best over-
   the-counter painkiller for burn pain,
   including sunburn.

   But if you have nothing with which
to specifically manage the burn, or if you're
hesitant to deal with it, don't mess with the
burn. It's not the best management plan,
but a burn's surface, without your help, will
dry into a scab-like covering that provides a
significant amount of protection.

SUNBURN

*Sunburn damage results
from the ultraviolet rays
of the sun and not from
the heat of the sun. But
the burn should still be
managed as described in
this chapter. Several steps
can be taken to pre-
vent sunburn, including
sunscreens, sunblocks,
tightly-woven cloth-
ing, brimmed hats, and,
of course, avoidance of*

OTHER THINGS YOU CAN DO

Keep the burned person as comfortable as possible. Keep the extensively burned person warm. If significant skin is lost, so will be the ability to maintain adequate core temperature. A drop in the body's core temperature is bad. Also have the person drink as much fluid as he will tolerate, unless he complains of nausea. To further protect against dehydration, treat nausea to allay vomiting, if possible.

BLISTERS ON FEET

The fluid-filled bubble of a blister on your foot is a mild partial-thickness burn caused by the heat of friction. Instead of rubbing sticks together (SEE CHAPTER 3), you're rubbing your foot against your boot. The friction produces a separation of the tough outer layer of skin from the sensitive inner layer. Fluid rushes in to fill the space between the layers of skin.

Blisters probably heal best—or at least safest—if you sit with your foot propped up for a few days, but you probably want to keep moving. You don't want a blister to pop inside a dirty sock inside a dirty boot, so the best wilderness medicine is to drain the blister in a controlled setting. Wash the site thoroughly. In a flame, sterilize the tip of a knife or safety pin, or wipe a sharp point with alcohol. Carefully slice the blister open and let it drain completely. Leaving the roof of the blister intact decreases pain and speeds healing. If the roof has been rubbed away when you discover the injury, treat the wound initially as you would any other: clean it and keep it clean to prevent infection.

After draining, you want to reduce the friction on that area as much as possible while keeping the foot in action. Many techniques and products are available for treating a deflated blister, some of the products specifically made and marketed for blister treatment—and some of them work well. A simple and proven although improvised technique involves creating a moleskin or molefoam "donut" to surround the blister site, then filling the hole of the "donut" with a glob of gooey ointment—a sort of jelly-filled donut. Any ointment will work. A liberal application of tincture of benzoin compound on the skin before the moleskin will greatly increase its stick-to-it-ness. A second patch of moleskin or a strip of tape over the filled donut will keep the ointment in place. A product called 2nd Skin works as well or better than moleskin to reduce friction over a deflated blister. 2nd Skin can be used to fill a "donut," or placed over the deflation site and held in place with moleskin or tape.

It's best, though, to prevent a blister from forming. Of critical importance is boot fit. It doesn't matter how expensive or fancy your boots are if the fit is poor. When purchasing new boots, fit your boots while wearing the socks that will be worn in them—with two pairs, if that's your plan. Boots that fit properly and that have been broken in go a long way toward preventing blisters. Keeping feet cool and dry is also important. Take frequent breaks with boots off. Wear a thin, nonslip liner sock that wicks moisture away from feet and into a thicker outer sock.

If a "hot spot"—a sore, red spot—develops at a prime blister site, stop and cover the area with tape, moleskin, or 2nd Skin before the blister has a chance to form. Moleskin conforms to the shape of feet better when cut into strips or ovals, instead of laying down a wide piece that inevitably refuses to go flat. Once again, tincture of benzoin compound applied first will help keep the tape or moleskin from peeling off when feet start sweating. Without tape or moleskin, benzoin alone can be applied to the skin to prevent blisters. Benzoin hardens protectively over the outer layer of skin.

EVACUATION GUIDELINES FOR BURNS

While not a matter of urgency, patients with burns that hinder the ability to participate in and/or enjoy the outdoor experience should be evacuated. Superficial burns, even extensive ones, rarely require evacuation. Partial thickness burns covering less than 10 percent TBSA should receive a doctor's care, but seldom warrant rapid evacuation. Full thickness burns need definitive medical care to heal best, but do not usually require rapid evacuation unless they are extensive or the victim's overall condition warrants it. Partial and full thickness burns covering 10 to 15 percent TBSA call for a rapid evacuation. Partial and full thickness burns covering more than 15 percent TBSA are a threat to life, requiring an evacuation as rapid as possible. Any serious burn to the face should be considered for rapid evacuation, as well as deep burns to genitals, armpits, hands, and/or feet. Circumferential burns around arms or legs also warrant immediate evacuation.

APPENDIX A

CHARRED BITS AND FLAMING PIECES

IN ANSWER TO SEVERAL BURNING QUESTIONS:

WHY DOES THE SMOKE FROM A CAMPFIRE SEEM TO BLOW INTO YOUR FACE NO MATTER WHERE YOU SIT OR HOW MANY TIMES YOU CHANGE POSITIONS AROUND THE FIRE?

Your body blocks the flow of fresh air drawn to the flames. You are then creating a low air pressure area with your body, and the warm smoke moves toward the lowest air pressure. With no wind, no matter where you sit in relation to the fire, the smoke will be drawn toward you.

WHO INVENTED THE MATCH?

It all got started back in 1669 when phosphorus was discovered. Phosphorus, in its white form, is an element that will spontaneously burst into flame when exposed to air. Phosphorus is also very poisonous. It can, however, be converted into red phosphorus, a much more stable form even though still poisonous.

In 1680 the Irish physicist Robert Boyle (of Boyle's Law fame) coated a small piece of paper with white phosphorus and a little piece of wood with sulfur. When he rubbed the wood against the paper, fire erupted. But that was as far as his interest took him.

It wasn't until 1827 that the first real match appeared. John Walker, an English chemist, coated the end of a stick with antimony sulfide, potassium chlorate, gum, and starch. After the chemicals dried, he could strike the coated stick anywhere and it would start to burn. Due to the fact that Walker's matches would flame up very easily, often when no one wanted them to, they were justifiably considered dangerous. They also smelled terrible when they burned. Even so, a man named Samuel Jones successfully marketed Walker's matches, calling them "Lucifers." Three years later, in 1830, a French chemist named Charles Suria made a match with white phosphorus. Suria's matches did not stink, but the white phosphorus made people sick. Some of them died. Suria was not very successful marketing his match.

In 1855 Johan Edvard Lundstrom, a Swede, patented the safety match. He put red phosphorus on sandpaper on the outside of a box and the rest of the chemicals on the match head. The match would only work when struck against the special surface on the box—it smelled okay, and nobody got sick since very little phosphorus was burned. This was a huge step forward.

But another big step was taken in 1910, when the Diamond Match Company patented the first nonpoisonous match in the United States. The Diamond match used a safe chemical called sesquisulfide of phosphorus. The Diamond Match Company is still very successfully selling matches today.

WHAT IS THE MAXIMUM TEMPERATURE THAT A WOOD-FUELED FIRE CAN REACH?

A campfire typically burns at between 900 and 1,200 degrees Fahrenheit at its hottest. Build the fire in a well-made stove and you can get the heat up to 1,600 degrees Fahrenheit. Fire in a furnace with forced air will get quite a bit hotter.

WHAT DOES THE WORD "CURFEW" HAVE TO DO WITH FIRE?

"Curfew," to us the time to be safely at home, came to English from the French "to cover." To speakers of English, "curfew" was originally 1) the metal cover that was often laid over hot coals to keep them alive until morning, and later 2) the signal given to bank the fire for the night.

DOES A FIRE BURNING IN, SAY, A 20-DEGREE WINTER SETTING PRODUCE THE SAME AMOUNT OF HEAT AS A SIMILAR FIRE BUILT IN A 70-DEGREE SUMMER SETTING?

Theoretically, yes. But a fire on a cold winter day will take longer to reach maximum temperature, and you may not feel the heat as much since the cold air is sucking up a lot of the heat.

HOW OLD DO TREES GET?

It depends on the species and the habitat. Trees of the same species that get plenty of water, proper nutrition, and freedom from fires and disease, will live a lot longer than their cousins that don't. As examples, maples are estimated to live for 80 to 250 years, chestnuts for 100 to 300 years, oaks for 300 to 600 years, and bald cypresses for 600 to 1,200 years. The oldest trees on Earth, however, are bristlecone pines. They are perhaps the oldest life on Earth. Some bristlecone pines in California's White Mountains, a part of the Sierra Nevada range, have reached 4,600 years. They were growing before the pyramids of Egypt were built. How long can a tree live? Nobody knows, but it has been suggested by some experts that, given ideal conditions, a bristlecone pine tree might live for 40,000 years!

When a tree is cut down, you can tell the age of the tree by counting the growth rings on the surface of the cut end. There will usually be one ring for each growing season. Not a precise science—occasionally a tree will develop two rings in one year—but counting the rings gives you a really good idea of the tree's age. Then look carefully: each ring typically shows two colors—a lighter color for less-dense growth early in the growing season, a darker color for more-dense growth later in the growing season. And the rings will not be the same width. A season with little water and nutrition will make a ring narrower than a season with abundant water and nutrition.

If you should ever kill a tree to burn it, you'll be killing a lot of history.

HOW CLOSE CAN YOU SIT NEXT TO A CAMPFIRE WITHOUT GETTING BURNED OR BURNING YOUR CLOTHES?

Depends on a lot of variables. How dry is your skin? How dry are your clothes? Things have to dry out before they ignite. You can sit a lot closer to a new fire fueled with damp wood than a full-on blaze fueled with very dry wood. Sit close enough for skin comfort. If you're too hot, you're too close. Clothes should feel warm but not hot. If they feel hot, move back.

HOW MUCH WOOD EXISTS ON EARTH?

Today trees cover about 20% of the land surface of this planet, and make up about 90% of the total terrestrial biomass. But those numbers are shrinking dramatically. Due to the fact that so many products are made of wood, the average American uses wood equal to 1 tree 16 to 18 inches in diameter and 100 feet tall every year. And that is just in the United States. Don't just use trees—go plant a tree!

SHOULD EXTREMELY CHILLED OR FROZEN SKIN EVER BE EXPOSED TO THE DIRECT HEAT OF A CAMPFIRE?

Never. Cold skin burns more easily than warm skin because there is reduced circulation in that area of the body. In addition, cold skin doesn't feel the heat as much, so you can burn without realizing you're burning. Warm cold flesh with skin-to-skin contact before exposing it to the heat of a fire. Warm frozen skin in water heated to 104 to 108 degrees Fahrenheit, wrap it in clean cloth or gauze, and find a doctor.

IS FIRE A FORM OF MATTER?

Matter is anything that has mass and occupies space. Fuel, therefore, is matter. Oxygen, too, is matter. A fire's flame is a mixture of gases—oxygen, carbon dioxide, water vapor, vaporized fuel, other stuff—so flame is matter. Light and heat, on the opposite side of the coin, are forms of energy. Light and heat are not matter.

ON A WINDLESS DAY, WHAT MAKES ONE FIRE'S SMOKE LIFT UP AND AWAY WHILE ANOTHER FIRE'S SMOKE CURLS AND LINGERS?

The barometric pressure. Low air pressure allows warm smoke to rise freely, and high air pressure "presses" it down, hugging it to the ground.

WHAT IS A "STORMPROOF" LIGHTER?

In a "stormproof" lighter, a piezo spark, created by a little hammer striking a small piece of quartz, ignites butane in an internal burning chamber. The flame heats up a wire coil. The heated coil both ignites and diffuses the gas, resulting in an intensely hot and highly wind-resistant flame from the port of the lighter. Some models, such as Brunton's Helios, will burn in winds of 80 miles per hour, and the Helios is waterproof when the lighter is closed.

APPENDIX B

GLOSSARY

ASH: the unburnable materials left after wood burns, such as potassium and calcium.

BIOMASS: the total of all the living and dead organic material in a given area.

CHAR: the carbon left after wood burns.

COMBUSTION: the rapid oxidation of organic material when that material ignites and burns, producing heat and light.

CROWN FIRE: a fire that climbs from the ground to the tops of trees, the most destructive type of wildland fire.

FIRE DRILLS: any of several tools for igniting a fire by creating heat from friction, such as bow drills and hand drills.

FIRE LAY: the arrangement of fuel for a fire, such as a teepee or star.

FIRE PISTON: a tool for generating heat to start a fire by rapidly slamming a piston into a cylinder.

FIRE STRIKERS: any of several tools used to ignite a fire by showering sparks on tinder, such as sparks from steel against flint.

FIRE TRIANGLE: a symbol for the three components—heat, oxygen, fuel—necessary for fire.

FIRE WHIRLS: rapidly rising spirals of hot air created by a raging wildfire.

FLAMMABILITY: the ease with which a fuel ignites and burns.

FLASH POINT: the temperature at which a material ignites and burns.

FUEL: all combustible material.

FUEL LOAD: all the potentially combustible material in a given area, usually expressed as tons per acre.

GROUND FIRE: wildfire that involves grasses and other low-lying vegetation.

HOTSHOT: a wildland firefighter who assaults the blaze via a ground attack.

KRUMMHOLZ: trees that grow in "islands," stunted and warped by severe conditions above normal treeline, typically fir and spruce.

OXIDATION: to combine with oxygen.

PYROTECHNOLOGY: the use of fire to create products other than heat and light, such as tools.

SEROTINOUS: tree description that usually indicates a seed-bearing cone that remains closed until an event such as fire stimulates seed dispersal.

SMOKE JUMPER: a wildland firefighter who parachutes into a remote fire site to assault the blaze.

SURFACE FIRE: wildfire that involves grasses, other low-lying vegetation, and the trunks of trees.

WILDFIRE: a highly destructive and uncontrolled fire.

WILDLAND FIRES: all fires that burn in wildlands, controlled or uncontrolled.

APPENDIX C
RESOURCES

Atwill, Lionel. "Thirty Years a Survivor." New York, NY: *Field & Stream*, August 1999.

Auerbach, Paul S., editor. *Wilderness Medicine*, Fourth Edition. St. Louis, MO: Mosby, Inc., 2001.

Brown, Tom. *Tom Brown's Field Guide to Wilderness Survival*. New York, NY: Berkley Books, 1983.

Cole, D. N., and J. Dalle-Molle. "Managing campfire impacts in the backcountry." Ogden, UT: *USDA Forest Service, Intermountain Forest and Range Experiment Station*, Research Paper INT-135, 1982.

Duffin, Gerry and Chauna. *The Dutch Oven Resource*. Logan, UT: Camp Chef, 2005.

Gurte, Ross W. "Forest Fires and Forest Health." Washington, DC: *Congressional Research Service Report*, July 1995.

Hampton, Bruce, and David Cole. *Soft Paths: How to Enjoy the Wilderness Without Harming It*. Mechanicsburg, PA: Stackpole Books, 1995.

Jamison, Richard and Linda. *Woodsmoke: Collected Writings on Ancient Living Skills*. Birmingham, AL: Menasha Ridge Press, 1994.

Lemon, Greg. "Fire on the mountain: unfettered flames an effective tool for wilderness management." Hamilton, MT: *Ravalli Republic*, August 18, 2004.

London, Jack. *To Build a Fire and Other Stories*. New York, NY: Bantam Books, 1986.

Maclean, Norman. *Young Men and Fire*. Chicago, IL: University of Chicago Press, 1992.

McGivney, Annette. *Leave No Trace: A Guide to the New Wilderness Etiquette*. Seattle, WA: The Mountaineers Books, 1998.

McPherson, John and Geri. *Naked into the Wilderness: Primitive Wilderness Living & Survival Skills*. Randolph, KS: Prairie Wolf, 1993.

Mills, Sheila. *The Outdoor Dutch Oven Cookbook*. New York, NY: McGraw-Hill/Ragged Mountain Press, 1997.

Olson, Sigurd F. *The Singing Wilderness*. New York, NY: Alfred A. Knopf, Inc., 1956.

Pyne, Stephen J. *Fire: A Brief History*. Seattle, WA: University of Washington Press, 2001.

Pyne, Stephen J. *Fire in America: A Cultural History of Wildland and Rural Fire*. Seattle, WA: University of Washington Press, 1997.

Pyne, Stephen J. *World Fire: The Culture of Fire on Earth*. Seattle, WA: University of Washington Press, 1995.

Pliny the Elder. *Natural History*, book 36, 159, the Loeb translation. Cambridge, MA: Harvard University Press, 1962.

Rehder, J. E. *The Mastery and Uses of Fire in Antiquity*. Montreal and Kingston, Canada: McGill-Queen's University Press, 2000.

Rutstrum, Calvin. *The New Way of the Wilderness*. New York, NY: The Macmillan Company, 1958.

Search and Rescue Survival Training, AF Regulation 64-4, Volume 1. Washington, DC: Department of the Air Force, 1985.

Snow, Gordon. *Safe and Sound: How Not to Get Lost in the Woods and How to Survive if You Do*. Fredericton, New Brunswick, Canada: Goose Lane, 1997.

Tilton, Buck. *Wilderness First Responder*, Second Edition. Guilford, CT: The Globe Pequot Press, 2004.

Whelan, Robert J. *The Ecology of Fire*. Cambridge, UK: Cambridge University Press, 1995.

Whelen, Colonel Townsend, and Bradford Angier. *On Your Own in the Wilderness*. Harrisburg, PA: The Stackpole Company, 1958.

White, Linda. *Cooking on a Stick: Campfire Recipes for Kids*. Salt Lake City, UT: Gibbs Smith, 1996.

Wiseman, John. *The SAS Survival Handbook*. London, UK: Harvill, 1986.

INDEX